Outdoor Mosaic

Outdoor Mosaic

ORIGINAL WEATHER-PROOF DESIGNS TO BRIGHTEN ANY EXTERIOR SPACE

Emma Biggs and Tessa Hunkin

Trafalgar Square Publishing

First published in the United States of America in 2001
by Trafalgar Square Publishing
North Pomfret, Vermont 05053

Printed and bound in China

This book was conceived and produced by
Breslich & Foss Ltd., London

ISBN 1 57076 196 5

Library of Congress Catalog Card Number: 00 110715

10 9 8 7 6 5 4 3 2 1

The publishers would like to thank the following agencies for
permission to reproduce images in this book: *The Art Archive* Villa
Casale, Sicily 7; (Dagli Orti) Basilica in Aquileia 40–41; (Dagli Orti)
National Anthropological Museum, Mexico City 72; *The Bridgeman
Art Library* Basilica in Herakleia Lynkestis 25; Villa Pia, Vatican City
57; (Lauros-Giraudon) Musee Lapidaire, Vienna 86–7; *Mosaic
Workshop* 43, 54, 55, 88, 103; *Raw Vision Magazine* 75; *Scala* Museo
delle Terme, Rome 8; Villa Casale, Sicily 24; Basilica in Aquileia 42;
Khirbat al Mafjar 56–7; Villa di Castello, Florence 64; Parco Guell,
Barcelona 74; Museum of the City, Barcelona 88. *Chris Simpson*
Moroccan zelige table 9.

All other photography by Shona Wood and copyright
© Breslich & Foss 2001.

The authors would also like to thank all those individuals who gave
permission for their mosaics to be photographed. Special thanks
are due to West Dean College & Gardens, Chichester, West Sussex
(www.westdean.org.uk) for permission to photograph on location:
13, 14, 15, 17, 19, 20, 21, 22, 23 (top), 80, 82, 83. The Gardens are
open daily from March to October. (Emma Biggs is a Short Course
tutor at the College.)

CONTENTS

6
Introduction
A guide for all types of garden and exterior space. Sources of inspiration.

9
Chapter 1
Tables
Patio Table
Cow-parsley Table
Ceramic Occasional Table
Rod Table

25
Chapter 2
Paths and Pavements
Animal Paving Stones
Mosaic Pavement
Greenhouse Path
Mosaic Inserts
Cast Slabs

41
Chapter 3
Mosaic and Water
Bird Bath
Mosaic Bridge
Pond Surround
Fountain

57
Chapter 4
Wall Mosaics
Colour Wall
Ceramic Mosaic Panel
Found Objects Panel
Charybdis
Icarus
Texture Panel

73
Chapter 5
Objects and Sculptures
Glass Mosaic Planter
Mosaic Head
Mythical Animal

87
Chapter 6
Conservatories and Porches
Translucent Panel
Number Panel
Entrance Porch
Echo and Narcissus

106
Chapter 7
Technical Information
Common Problems
Materials
Tools

114
Basic Methods

126
List of Suppliers and Places to Visit

INTRODUCTION

This book is a guide to using mosaic outside, or in parts of the home that lead outside: areas such as a conservatory, a garden room or the threshold to a house or apartment. It also looks at solutions to a common problem – a blank depressing exterior wall overlooked from within the home that even the horticulturally gifted cannot salvage. These difficult areas are an opportunity for someone with imagination to transform with mosaic!

Mosaic can be extremely diverse in appearance and sensibility: it can be highly colored and intense, or employ a restrained and natural palette of colors. It can be textural or reflective, used on walls or floors, or tables. It can look urban and contemporary, or ancient and timeless. It is endlessly adaptable and a first effort can look as lively (sometimes more lively) as the work of an experienced mosaicist. Mosaic projects are also very enjoyable to do.

Seeing something attractive through a window rather than editing out the view makes a surprising difference to how you feel about a room. The techniques involved in making exterior mosaics are largely similar to the techniques used indoors, but the preparatory work, some of the adhesives and the surfaces onto which they are fixed may be different. It is also important, as we stress throughout the book, to use colors and materials suitable for an external context. This means thinking about the weather, or at least thinking about how the materials you want to use relate to the climate in which you want to use them.

This book is divided into chapters dealing with different topics – tables, for example, or paths and pavements. Every chapter begins with an introduction that puts the subject into a historical context, then describes the kind of work people are doing today. For example, the chapter on objects and sculptures discusses the Aztec turquoise mosaics found in Mexico, then goes on to discuss the work of a contemporary artist, Nek Chand. Each chapter discusses examples of mosaics we have made. Some are more complex than others, but the aim isn't necessarily that you should copy them. We discuss issues involved in each design and considerations behind the choice of materials. We also point out anything typical of the example.

We don't imagine that every reader will want to make a series of projects identical to the ones presented here, but should you wish to make something similar, or use the technique to create your own design, the technical section and the instructions will enable you to do so. In addition to professional advice on designing mosaics, the book contains a series of boxes that contain useful tips plus information on issues you're likely to encounter when working outside, such as the problems water can cause. The box on lettering might be helpful in planning a sign for your house – an obvious but very satisfying project to tackle as a beginner. Following the technical section there is a description of useful tools and materials, a list of suppliers and suggestions of mosaic sites you might like to visit. We hope you find the book useful and helpful in avoiding the kinds of mistakes we made in order to be able to write it!

CHAPTER I
TABLES

It is surprising how quickly a new mosaic gives the impression that it has always been there. It can be frustrating to work on something for months and find people fail to notice it, even if a sense of timelessness seems fitting in a garden. You can ensure your work comes in for close scrutiny, though, by giving it a practical rather than simply a decorative function — that of a table.

It is likely that some older mosaics we see used as tables were not originally designed with that purpose in mind. For example, there are technically astonishing micromosaic tables, made from "filamenti" or tiny glass rods, cut and laid to make designs of such detail you could be forgiven for not realising they were mosaic at all. In order to understand what a technical feat the work is, it needs to be examined at close quarters. Micromosaics were at their most popular in the eighteenth century, and the center of their production was the Vatican workshops with their vast stores of material and unrivalled quantities of colors. These workshops still produce micromosaics today — largely reproductions of famous mosaics made for tourists. Micromosaics are also produced in Russia, but the product made is more likely to adorn a tiny decorative box than a large functional table for obvious practical reasons. In both cases the designs tend to be conservative, making recognisable references to an earlier tradition, sometimes mosaic, sometimes painting. Although we do not discuss how to make micromosaic in this book, the techniques are simple enough. You can use either the direct or indirect method — whichever method you choose it will certainly be slow-going.

Another form of mosaic which has become very popular in recent years is Moroccan tile mosaic, or zelige. (This word is spelt in many different ways!) Here intricate shapes are cut from glazed tiles (sometimes in combination with unglazed tiles) by craftsmen working with sharp mosaic hammers. As mosaicists, we have tried endlessly to reproduce this technique, but without luck. Shapes that are quite impossible to make using traditional mosaic materials — internal angles for example — seem to be cut easily, perhaps partly because of the soft tile body. The glazes vary slightly in tone and density, giving a natural appearance to the colors that works well outside.

PATIO TABLE

The advantage of this low table is that it acts as a table and a bench simultaneously, so you can sit in the sun with books, newspapers and a cool drink in hand. It was made for a small roof terrace that is surrounded by buildings of various sizes, shapes and materials. At night their dark silhouettes are made lively by shining rectangles of light from the windows. This was the starting point for the design.

The table combines diverse materials in a structured way, just as the buildings do, and the size of the tiles creates an impression of depth. Larger pieces were laid in the foreground at the bottom of the table; the pieces become smaller towards the top. But the structure does include an element of chance as the pieces were laid without additional cutting, just as they were found.

The color range is limited to blacks and grays that are sympathetic to the muted colors of the urban surroundings. However, in summer the table is framed by pots of vividly colored nasturtiums, poppies, lilies and lobelia. It isn't easy to compete with this natural technicolor, so instead the monochrome mosaic is made lively by the use of reflective materials. The tiles are sometimes used upside down so the metallic leaf can be seen through its glass backing. The blue-backed silver and the green-backed gold tiles have the virtue of intense reflective color as well as depth.

Surface quality is also used to help distinguish one area (or building) from another. Some marble is unpolished, which makes even the unglazed ceramic look less matte by comparison; some is incised with the diagonal marks of the saw. A certain amount of polished black marble was used and over time the surface has weathered to a less shiny finish. The only remaining highly polished element is a piece of black granite, a material hard enough to be unaffected by the weather. One attractive feature of using unpolished material outside is the transforming effect of the rain. This table becomes much darker with a sharper contrast against the shining glass inserts, becoming a night-time version of the design.

The table was fixed onto mineral fiber board which was dropped into the metal angle that forms the table base. (The same principle as the Rod Table.) It is obviously important that a table should have a flat surface, which can be difficult when using materials of varying thicknesses. The easiest way to achieve a level finish is to make the mosaic by the indirect (or reverse) method.

When the design is complete and dry, pregrout the mosaic. Sponge the grout off the back, leaving it only in the joints between tiles. Mix some adhesive to a stiff consistency and smooth it across the tiles until you achieve a level surface. (This method is sometimes known as "buttering the back".) Trowel adhesive, as you would normally, onto the backing board. Place the mosaic into the adhesive, paper side up. Now tap the whole mosaic with a small board and light hammer, to achieve a level surface. Wet the paper, leave for ten minutes to absorb water, checking at intervals to ensure the paper has not dried out. Peel off the paper. If any tiles have dipped lower than their neighbours, hook them out and re-lay, making sure you put additional adhesive behind them. Finally, regrout the table and sponge clean in the usual way.

COW-PARSLEY TABLE

This table is designed to stand beside a chair, and can be moved around the garden according to the time of day or the season. It is light, which makes it easily moveable, yet solid enough not to be upended by a gust of wind.

The design comes from a member of the Umbelliferae family of plants, named after the Latin word for sunshade because the flower heads radiate out from a single point like the spokes of an umbrella. Many members of this family are grown as garden plants, for example astrantia or melancholy gentleman. Some, such as caraway, parsley, fennel, coriander, parsnip and carrot, are cultivated in herb and vegetable gardens. Others, like deadly hemlock or cow-parsley, flourish in hedgerows and fields. They all share the same distinctive arrangement of flowers on which this design is based. As tables are used from all sides, the design must work from any angle, which makes pattern an ideal subject. Representational subject matter like the cow parsley can be stylized and used for its patterned qualities, as this design demonstrates.

The flowers are executed in a combination of glass and unglazed ceramic. The idea for the design came from looking at a mosaic material only recently available: circular ceramic tiles made in two shades of white. These have been cut into segments and mixed with glass tiles to create the flickering white roundels. Careful examination of a cow-parsley plant will reveal that each individual flower head has a spoked structure leading to tiny florets. This structure is suggested by the radiating joints in the mosaic. The variety of whites lends a delicacy to the flowers that suggests the lace-like complexity of the plant.

If you want to stylize from nature when designing a mosaic, it is important to find a form that conveys the character of the subject while using the scale and qualities of the medium. This table is small, so the plant has been simplified to ensure the mosaic doesn't look fussy. The design could work on a much larger scale by repeating the elements to represent several flower heads.

Like the white, the green making up the stalks is used in a variety of tones that contribute to the flickery effect. The background is a mixture of black, gray and green, laid in concentric circles softening the dramatic tonal contrast with the flowers.

To keep the weight down, this table should be made on a wooden board, such as exterior ply or MDF, with a hardwood frame. It can be made using the direct method with an aliphatic wood glue such as Titebond, but it is easier to achieve a flat surface using the indirect method. The mosaic should be grouted a dark color to unite the dark colors of the background and accentuate the radiating joints between white tiles that are important to the design. A dark color of paint or stain, relating to the background color, works well on the table base and frame.

CERAMIC OCCASIONAL TABLE

The design for this table is based on a section of tree trunk. It is constructed in a series of circles, to remind the viewer of growth rings. The idea is given a visual twist though, as the lines have two points of orientation. Black lines emanate from the center and cream lines radiate to the center. The mosaic was designed for a setting where there is quite a lot of flint, and the colors are intended to have something flint-like about them. The restrained palette makes the table equally suitable for any part of a colorful garden.

The tabletop design follows a single rule, with regular, careful spacing of gaps between tiles. (Rhythmic spacing creates a feeling of harmony – it helps to unite diverse elements, like the time signature of a piece of music.) The design is simple, but complex enough to be interesting. It takes a while to spot the rule organising the tiles, which run in rings of varied width but join one another precisely. The time it takes to discover this rule is what gives the design interest. Good design has to strike a balance between the simple and concise, and restraint to the point of boredom.

This mosaic has a visual surprise: the white line that runs across it. In a black and cream mosaic, the white is a curiosity, and gives the design piquancy. Even a tiny amount of white acts as an intensifier, and enables the eye to read the pearl (cream) as a color.

The table has been grouted gray, so the black and cream material is broken up evenly. A lighter grout would have united the pale ceramic and thrown the black material out of balance, and a dark grout would have broken up the pale areas and drawn together the black ones. (Do bear in mind that dark grout can stain pale-colored ceramic.) This would have given a different impression of how the design was weighted. Have a look at the accompanying illustrations and note the effect the grout colors have. It can be effective to weight one area of a design as a contrast to its surroundings so, although this design was treated in the same way across the whole mosaic, it would have been possible to use two grout colors.

The table has a hardwood frame and a marine ply base. Both materials have similar ways of reacting to heat and cold, making it less likely that the grout joint around the edge would crack in extreme weather.

ROD TABLE

This contemporary-looking table is made from marble – a material that has been used by mosaicists since antiquity. Part of the process of cutting cubes (the name given to small marble mosaic tiles) involves cutting larger tiles into rods. The cubes are then cut from these long thin pieces. Marble works well outside, and this table design uses the material in all its stages, aiming to derive color and textural impact from the contrast between them.

The close tones of carrara (white marble) and botticino (creamy colored marble) are attractive when combined. Carrara can be very gently streaked with gray, and botticino often looks flickery in comparison. The characteristically mossy looking botticino is known as "fiorito" (flowered). Fiorito often contains pale, whitish marks. Creamier in color and less mottled, it is known as botticino classico. These pale materials are used in contrast to darker ones, such as blue granite from South America and green alpine marble, giving drama to the design.

There is contrast of scale thanks to the range of sizes of material used, from a half tile, to rods, cubes and riven cubes. Finally there is textural contrast between the open face of the stone and the polished marble. This decision is not made on aesthetic grounds alone, as a polish does increase the stone's protection against potentially staining materials, such as wine and oil. Stone has an open face when it has been "riven", or cut through to expose its natural inner color. This face is porous, and stone sealant should be applied before the table is used. The slightly uneven surface of the stone is pleasing to touch, and the restrained way it is used – bound on all sides by flat material – prevents it threatening the stability of glasses and tableware.

The mosaic was fixed with cement-based adhesive to a mineral board called Pyroc, which is thermally stable. This is important because, if you make an exterior table, you are likely to encounter problems with thermal movement. Where two adjoining surfaces – such as the steel perimeter of a table, and the wooden base on which the mosaic is fixed – respond differently to heat and cold, any attempt to grout them into a single entity is likely to result in the junction between them cracking. If the table is jointed tightly and subject to extremes of movement, the mosaic will release pressure by expanding along the weakest point, which may be its bond with the table base. No one wants the hard work and expense of making a mosaic to end up in a thousand pieces, so it is worth taking these problems seriously.

We have found that the only solution to uniting materials that react in conflicting ways to heat and cold is to allow them to move independently. We no longer grout them as if they were a single unit. Instead the mosaic is fixed to whatever sheet material from which the tabletop is made, and this is laid into the table base. The joint between the frame and the tabletop is left ungrouted. Water may fall into this joint, but it can drain away without causing damage.

Inspiration is not a finite resource and it doesn't come to those who don't need it: the process of working produces it. It is possible to be lucky and come across something by accident, but most creative discoveries arrive from working at a problem until a solution is found. The formula for creativity is to put in plenty of work and be prepared to experiment.

Occasionally a fresh idea is what is needed to kick start the imagination, and nature is an endlessly rich resource. The decorative arts (which is what mosaic is) have always revealed how people look at nature. Sometimes it has been a nostalgic look – for example the wishful medievalism of William Morris, working at a time when nature was under siege by industry; sometimes it has been celebratory, such as the scientific fascination with nature in the 1950s. Today artists take genuine pleasure in using materials that seem to express a sense of place, things found in the garden, or found by the mosaic maker. Anyone who has looked at a mosaic book will have noticed the enormous popularity of fish with mosaic makers. Perhaps it is the visual relationship – the scaley look of mosaic – but it may also come from an appreciation of an untamed element of the natural world.

FLINT AND STONE WALL

It can often be helpful to study the way others have used natural materials. It is easy to steal good ideas like the one seen here. This summerhouse wall has a wonderful contrast of smooth and textured surfaces. The stone is absorbent of light and the broken face of the knapped flint is reflective. Tiny shards have been pushed into the mortar between the flints. The contrast of scale and surface is appealing.

SUMMERHOUSE FLOOR

This is an idea that would not be so easy to steal, although it is an example of recycling with an interesting history. This summerhouse floor is made from a combination of knapped flints and horses' teeth, which create the white pattern on the floor. The teeth are reputed to have come from horses killed in the Napoleonic Wars.

BEACHCOMBER

These beachcombed items demonstrate that a restricted palette is not necessarily a boring one. The pebbles have a visual rhythm with their circular shapes and holes. Paring back the color allows you to be more expressive with form, texture and the graphic properties of the material.

CHAPTER 2
PATHS AND PAVEMENTS

Mosaic works well on the floor because it is both hardwearing and decorative. Some of the earliest floor mosaics were made as panels that could be moved around, and Julius Caesar is said to have taken them on his military campaigns. A tradition of mosaic paths and pavements spans centuries and it is not uncommon to find Roman mosaics laid one on top of the other, as you occasionally see linoleum laid today. Maybe the mosaic was damaged, or perhaps the owner just wanted a new, more fashionable design. The famous bikini-clad women in Piazza Armerina, Sicily are laid over an earlier floor, as are several mosaics at Fishbourne Roman Palace, near Chichester. It is a practice that continues even now: the mosaic entrance to London's Groucho Club was relaid above another when the door was restructured recently.

The earliest mosaic pavements were made from pebbles of contrasting colors with lead strips used to help to delineate areas. Contrast and clarity – issues discussed frequently in this book – are perennial concerns of mosaicists. Both polychromatic and black and white mosaics were common throughout the ancient world and these have had an enduring influence. When Mussolini made his ambitious Olympic bid in the 1930s, the vast sports complex included mosaic pavements. Mussolini had Imperial ambitions, and the pavements show, among other things, his troops going into Abyssinia. The stylistic model for this were the black and white mosaic

Baths of Neptune from Ostia Antica. Mussolini's huge decorative scheme in natural stone has a highly questionable political and moral content, but is nonetheless extremely impressive in scale and execution.

Unglazed ceramic, marble and other stone are all suitable as paving materials as they have more of an earthy, natural range of tones and colors than glass, which is less suitable for flooring being fragile and potentially slippery underfoot.

CAST SLABS

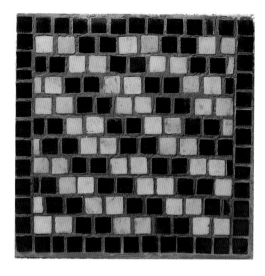

Cast slabs like the ones shown here are ideal for assembling a garden path or to act as a central feature on an empty area of lawn. The black and white marble cubes allow you to experiment with different kinds of patterns. Although you can cast into almost anything (we have even made circular paving slabs in a dish washing bowl!) it may be worth constructing a special casting tray. If the tray is well-looked after – taken to pieces and sealed before its first use – it may last forever. It can also be worth experimenting with the recipe for sand and cement mixtures and keeping a note of it for future reference. (We often inscribe the proportions of a successful mix together with the date, into the wet sand and cement.)

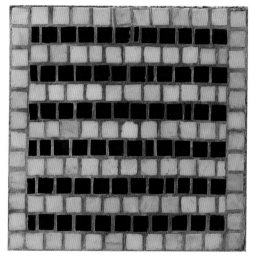

The slabs are all made from marble cubes, using similar colors. Don't let the time it may take between completing one slab and beginning another tempt you to use too diverse and contrasting a range of materials. The pavers may be effective individually, but it is important to bear in mind how they relate to one another.

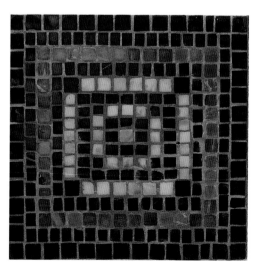

ANIMAL PAVING STONES

These little paving stones can be used to enliven various places in the garden, perhaps providing firm footing in an area of gravel or acting as stepping stones in a flowerbed or across a lawn.

The designs were inspired by Roman pavements, which often show the mythical Greek poet Orpheus playing his lyre surrounded by admiring creatures. In some examples the names of the animals are written into the mosaic. This is a nice touch because, by providing an extra aid to identification, it liberates the designs from a slavish accuracy. Some of the exotic animals are quite hard to recognize, but this is not surprising. Roman artists did not have access to wildlife encyclopedias to draw elephants and crocodiles from life would have been a dangerous business!

These four pavers are based on native English wildlife, but would look at home in any leafy garden. The attraction of Roman pavements is often found in the simplicity of the designs and the very limited range of colors. A creamy white background is usually used and the animals are rendered in the earthy tones available in the local stone.

In these little mosaics, black has been used as well to introduce contrast and variety but the creatures are described simply in tones of brown and gray. They are made of unglazed ceramic mosaic tiles, which are available in a range of muted colors, and that are easier to cut and work with than natural stone. The range of different background colors has meant that it is possible to use carefully positioned black and white in the animals without creating confusion: for instance the white front of the stoat reads against the black background while his little black eyes stand out against the white.

The textures and markings of the different creatures have been simplified into patterns generated by the shapes of the mosaic pieces. The pavers are, therefore, very easy to make but they also have an unfussy restraint that seems natural and elegant. The hedgehog's bristles are made of long thin pieces of alternating blacks and browns laid both to his outline and across his body to create an impression of ball-like roundness. The mottled breast of the thrush is a pattern of brown spots against gray, lightening to white at the front. The owl's back is a simple combination of checkerboard and stripes, while his face is framed by long thin pieces of alternating gray and white that suggest the radiating growth of feathers. The stoat does not have distinctive markings, but the texture of his fur is suggested by a checkerboard pattern of two tonally similar colors that enliven the surface and blend together to create an in-between color.

The backgrounds are made up of pieces of different sizes and laid with wide joints in a random way. The non-directional effect creates an interesting flat surface. This free technique of laying means that using very small pieces at edges and junctions can be avoided because the bonding can be adjusted in any way that is convenient. Equally, smaller modules can be introduced, as in the lettering, without creating an awkward effect. Using black and white, which are available in different ranges of ceramic, allows a greater variety in the size of the pieces. Different shades of white can be used to give a more natural effect by imitating the tonal variety found in stone and marble. The pieces are grouted in gray, which breaks up the black and white areas equally to give a balanced effect. The mid-tone of the gray is similar to that of the grays and browns used on the animals and therefore unites the creatures against the more fractured backgrounds.

These paving stones were made using the indirect method, which is easy to do when using unglazed ceramic as the material is exactly the same on both sides. Special care, however, must be taken with the lettering so that it reads correctly when fixed. With small mosaics you can draw the letters the correct way round on the shiny side of the brown paper then hold it up against a window pane and trace them through in reverse. The backing material for each paver is a thin and relatively light frostproof ceramic floor tile, but you can also use a pre-cast concrete paving slab. Remember that the edges of mosaics are vulnerable so the tiles need to be positioned flush with the surrounding ground surface.

Lettering can look very appealing in mosaic, but there are some common problems that can trip you up. This advice is not intended to deter experimentation, but to make your experiments more likely to succeed. Do invent your own lettering style, but keep in mind the need for clarity.

Incidentally, signs can be signs without lettering – just think of the Shell Oil Company logo. Again there are ancient precedents. Pompeii has several houses with *Cave Canem* mosaics on the threshold of the building. These mosaics of dogs tell the visitor to be on the alert and were intended to convey their meaning even to people who couldn't read.

The first issue is obvious, but surprisingly easy to forget. If you are working in reverse to make a sign or a house name, you must reverse the drawing. It is by seeing tell-tale back-to-front lettering that we know mosaicists centuries ago used the indirect method. Reversing a drawing also means reversing thick and thin lettering strokes. Signs become easier to read if you are consistent about which side of the letter is stressed.

When you draw up your design think about how to lay the background. Here (above) the background is straight laid. Another conventional treatment – running a line of mosaic around the outside of a letter – is elegant and can help to disguise oddities like the one that stands out here. (The mosaicist seems to have cut the white quarter tiles below the central black horizontal stroke of the A to a slightly bigger size than the rest. This mistake may have been caused by laying the black stroke before determining the position of the quarter tiles.)

Whether it is black on white or white on black, the contrast between these letters makes them legible. Lettering always involves a series of minute decisions. Here (below) the top bulge of the B rests on top of the lower one. It might have been more effective if both parts had sprung from the center equally, rather than one resting on the other. The best solution to a problem like this is consistency. If this treatment (a thicker upper bar and a tapering lower one) was repeated in other letters with similar characteristics – a D or a P, for example – it would be clear that the effect was not accidental.

Readable lettering requires careful color selection. The letter **E** (above) has color contrast, but no tonal contrast. Once grouted, similar tones fuse together becoming difficult to read. The only remedy for a problem like this is to use a grout of violently different tone, which can be rather jarring.

Lettering doesn't always have to be neatly executed to be readable. The style of letters **F** and **G** is chaotic, but the energy of the treatment gives them charm. Tonal contrast gives the piece clarity.

The hardest material from which to make lettering that is perfectly legible is mirror glass. It is reflective, and the reflections are distracting. Even the letters **M**, **N** and **O** seen below (cut and laid with great care) become difficult to read when reflecting movement. It is more sensible to use mirror tiles in a background rather than for the letters themselves.

MOSAIC PAVEMENT

This pavement was commissioned by the client as a present for his wife. A key part of the brief was that the mosaic should relate to the wife's interests, among which was an enthusiasm both for her garden and for the natural world. The mosaic was to be laid in the courtyard, around a fountain the client had built as an earlier gift.

It was important to think about a number of issues in producing a design, one of which was the relationship between the mosaic, the house and the garden. The house surrounded three sides of a courtyard, like an E-shape without the central bar. The mosaic would always be overlooked, so it had to make sense both at close range and at a distance. The courtyard was large, and the scale of the design had to relate to this architectural space. The budget was another consideration. The mosaic had to look effective without costing more than the client wished to spend. This wasn't merely a matter of choosing which material to use. It also involved deciding how complex the design should be (complicated designs take longer to produce) and choosing the size of the tiles (smaller tiles take longer both to cut and to lay). All of the above – scale, a sympathetic relationship to the surroundings and design clarity – are affected by color.

All colors have a relationship with, and are affected by, colors that surround them. Seasonal changes alter not only the appearance of the garden, but also the appearance of the mosaic. It is important to remember that a garden that is abundant and colorful when you lay a mosaic in summer may be transformed into a bleaker vista with the coming of winter. Using materials that relate in texture, finish, color, or scale to their environment, can make seasonal changes complement the design, rather than doing it a disservice.

The decision to have the mosaic echo the circular shape of the fountain rather than the rectangular shape of the courtyard was made easier by drawing both on a plan. A square or a rectangle had less visual impact than a circle; it also seemed better value for money. It is surprising how big a difference in area there is between a square and a circle that fits within it. It can make a lot of difference to the time it takes to make a mosaic.

How could a mosaic say something about the local environment and the wool trade? Although sheep were kept in East Anglia, the wool was woven elsewhere, made into bolts of cloth and carpets. A floor mosaic is like a scaled-up version of a woven fabric. Both require an

even tension (or, in the case of mosaic, spacing) and derive their designs from playing creatively with the basic unit: the woven stitch or the tile.

So making the mosaic look carpet-like was a way of making it express a sense of place. But what about the rest of the subject matter? Rugs and carpets often depict vegetation. It would have been possible to divide the design into twelve parts, each for a month, but it looked more appealing divided asymmetrically, and twelve sections seemed too pat an idea. Subdividing further, and varying the widths of the sections was a less geometrically formal approach. The repeated use of the almond shape (suggesting leaves, fish and seeds) unites the divided elements. The graphic, flat—lacking perspective—treatment of the vegetation is a contemporary approach. It also related better to the slight wobbliness of the fountain surround, and the randomness of the crazy paving into which the mosaic was laid.

If a design relies, as this does, on asymmetry, it is important to keep an eye on how the colors balance. Colors with high tonal contrast need to be dispersed throughout the design, rather than clustered in one area. The bands bordering the fountain, and the wider bands ringing the design, pick up colors used elsewhere, and help to prevent the design seeming oddly weighted. On a purely practical note, the tile size is .75 inches, but a cube of 2 inches was used to surround the mosaic, as it made a more elegant transition between the mosaic and the crazy paving.

GREENHOUSE PATH

This vitreous glass mosaic was made for a greenhouse path. It is easier to see the way the blues, grays and greens relate to their surroundings than the black and white tiles, but the garden features a lot of flint, which the mosaic echoes.

The starting point for this design was the fabric gingham: a cross weave of white and another color. The design experiments with distorting the pattern, changing the interweaving color, and slipping the module (the term for the way a design repeats) where the color changes to that of the section immediately above and the white dots no longer line up. Experiments like these are made to see what will happen, what the visual effect will be of inventing a rule then pushing it to its limit. In this case, the distortions seem to relate to those of nature: the way heat or moving water distorts an image.

There are one or two technical considerations to bear in mind. If you don't already have a path, it is probably easiest to employ a builder to construct one for you rather than attempting it yourself. There needs to be a good foundation of hardcore, on which to lay a sand and cement screed. (For further information about this see page 121 of the technical section.) This mosaic was made by the reverse method, and fixed with a flexible cement-based adhesive. It is important in locations where there are likely to be extreme variations in temperature, to use an adhesive that can withstand them. This is important, as heat leads the mosaic to expand and contract, often with dire consequences. The least of these can be cracking, which is often inevitable, unpredictable and best regarded as part of the ageing process. The worst can be the entire mosaic coming away from the base. Prevention is much easier than cure: make sure you use the right adhesive in the first place.

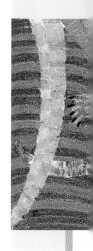

MOSAIC INSERTS

A sand and cement screed or a rendered wall can be attractive in their own right, but making a feature of such bare simplicity by including a decorative element reveals the bareness to be a choice, rather than an omission. In this example, a decorative strip is made from floor (or pavimento) gold and silver: some of the most expensive mosaic materials available. There is something pleasing about the contrast between the prestigious appearance of the gold and silver and the everyday appearance of the sand and cement that seems to enhance them both. The pleasurable contrast is not only in value, but also in appearance. The sand and cement is matte and light absorbent, with a slightly granular finish. The gold and silver are highly reflective and given depth by their colored transparent facings. Their glassy sheen contrasts not only with the sand and cement in which they are laid, but also with the cement slurry used to grout them.

Animals and birds make attractive subjects for outdoor mosaics. They look at home in natural surroundings and perhaps compensate for the increasing rarity of encounters with real wildlife. Making designs from animals can be approached in many different ways: creatures such as snakes and butterflies provide complex patterns and intense colors, but a lot of wildlife is without such showy visual appeal. Small brown animals and birds are, however, just as full of character and vitality and one design approach is to find a pose or attitude that is particularly characteristic. This can often be done by imagining an animal in motion and isolating a moment that conveys the way that it moves or the way that it holds itself when it suddenly hears something and stops to listen.

We are fortunate to live in an age in which drawings and photographs of animals are widely reproduced, but finding a suitable picture is only the beginning of the process of making a workable design. Even small living creatures are a miracle of complexity, and it would be impossible to convey in any medium their every detail. To make a design or a mosaic you must select the aspects that are significant and edit out the rest. This can be easier to achieve if you start from an image that is already simplified in some way. Black and white photographs make excellent source material because without color it is easier to concentrate on shape and form. These will be the key elements of the design and, without the need for an exact match, colors can be chosen to relate in terms of tone and hue. Black and white drawings fulfill a similar function whether found in natural history books or made yourself from photographs or life.

While all inspiration comes originally from our experience of the outside world, we have the power to transform it imaginatively into new and exciting images and forms. Elements from a variety of different sources can be combined to make stylized generic animals and birds. In these bird tiles (left), the forms are loosely based on long-legged wading birds but have been adapted to fit elegantly into the square shape of the tile.

CHAPTER 3
MOSAIC AND WATER

Mosaic is often used in close proximity to water, whether indoors in bathrooms and showers or outside around pools and fountains. Mosaic materials like vitreous glass and unglazed ceramic are unaffected by water even if fully submerged. They are therefore a very practical finish in wet areas. However, care must be taken with fixing and backing materials to insure that they are equally durable. Information and advice about suitable products is given in Chapter 7.

Mosaic can be visually sympathetic to water. The fractured nature of a mosaic has a relationship with the fractured reflections found on the surface of water. The eye pieces together the fragments to create a readable image. Many mosaic materials are light reflective and can be used in combination with matte surfaces to convey the complex patterns of reflectivity, light and shadow found in water.

Ancient mosaics often took the sea as their subject, depicting both native Mediterranean creatures and exotic mythical monsters. They are found in pavements of Roman ports such as Ostia Antica and Rimini, and decorating baths and private houses. In the early Christian world fish iconography acquired a new meaning – symbolizing Christ – so marine subjects appear in churches as well and are an example of the continuity between the classical and Christian traditions. The huge and beautiful pavement at the basilica in Aquileia (left) that dates from the fourth century AD, looks like a traditional Roman scene but it is actually illustrating the story of Jonah and the whale. This mosaic has another unique feature: it was uncovered only recently from beneath a medieval floor and over time it has subsided in places, leaving a gently undulating surface that accidentally but effectively mimics the waves of the sea.

In later church mosaics of the Byzantine and medieval periods, water is depicted in increasingly stylized ways. In scenes of the Baptism of Christ and Old Testament cycles of the creation of the oceans, horizontal lines of laying and the color blue are used to symbolize the idea of water rather than its appearance.

Today mosaics are generally used for more utilitarian purposes, such as covering swimming pools. Vitreous glass tiles were largely designed with this application in mind, and the paper-faced sheets provide a way to cover large areas relatively quickly. The range of pale blues available are the colors universally associated with pools, and the combinations of different shades sold as standard sheets represent a contemporary stylisation of "wateriness". Pools can, of course, provide opportunities for a more imaginative use of design and color, but locating mosaic pieces underwater presents some design constraints. Looking through a large body of water creates distortion because water diffracts light. The bottom of a pool will appear closer and otherwise unaffected, but the sides will be dramatically compressed and decoration below the water line will become invisible. The best locations for mosaic designs are, therefore, on the base of a pool or in a frieze above the water at the top of the side walls.

Water also reflects light, so designs need to be boldly conceived if they are to read clearly against the distractions of the glittering surface. A simple but striking approach is to break up the whole area into blocks of different colors to form a balanced composition. The more common solution is to set one or more feature panels into the surrounding plain tiling. Swimming pool companies sell a limited range of standard designs such as dolphin and compasses, but there are many more imaginative and personal options. In the Workshop we have made mermaids and sea monsters as well as boxing gloves for a champion heavy weight!

The chemicals added to pool water keep it beautifully clear, but you will find that other areas of standing water – such as ponds and fountains – may become muddy and prone to growth of algae. These problems can be overcome (see page 107 of the technical section), but they can also be avoided by locating your mosaic close to the water but not underneath it. Three of the projects in this chapter – a pond surround, a panel behind a fountain and a bridge over a pool – allow mosaic and water to be viewed together and are designed to exploit the interesting juxtaposition of color and reflectivity.

BIRD BATH

This is an extremely simple mosaic to make. The tiles are laid into a shallow terracotta bowl of the kind sometimes used to catch water from a much larger pot. Terracotta is very absorbent of water, but lining the inside of the bowl with mosaic has an effect similar to that of applying a glaze: it slows down the rate at which water is taken up by the body of the clay. The decoration on the bowl is sparing, and intended to suggest its function.

Two techniques have been used. The base was initially laid on paper, by the indirect method, then the mosaic on the flaring sides of the bowl was laid directly into the adhesive. In both cases, the terracotta was primed with PVA before the tiles were applied. These two techniques were used because each was the quickest and easiest way to fix the mosaic to the bowl. It is difficult to cut paper to a flaring curve, especially when the tiles are laid parallel to the rim as they are here, so this part of the mosaic was fixed directly. On the other hand, there is a risk, working onto a three dimensional form, of knocking tiles and breaking their bond with the adhesive. This makes it more sensible, when it is easy to do so, to lay tiles onto paper, and to fix a fragile mosaic all at once.

The tiles are "gemme": vitreous glass striated with metallic ore. Opinions differ about these tiles – some people love them, others find their appearance over-luxurious. The color shown here is the darkest blue available in the mosaic palette, which makes it useful to designers. You will notice that the tiles are laid off-set to one another. This is both a deliberate and a practical choice: it would be an extremely difficult job to cut the tiles so that the joints ran through throughout, and a mixture of the two is not a particularly pleasing effect. The tiles look better off-set, but even this effect is not labor-free. The ever-contracting circles mean joints will inevitably begin to meet. Your job is to keep them out of sync with one another, which can be done easily by cutting the odd three-quarter-length tile.

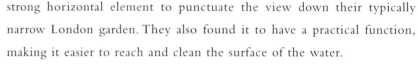

MOSAIC BRIDGE

This long, thin mosaic panel was designed to act as a bridge across a garden pond. It may seem eccentric to have a bridge over so small a piece of water, but the clients wanted to introduce a

strong horizontal element to punctuate the view down their typically narrow London garden. They also found it to have a practical function, making it easier to reach and clean the surface of the water.

The juxtaposition of mosaic and water presented an exciting brief, but the natural lushness of the surrounding plants presented severe visual competition. Petals and leaves are often slightly translucent and very strongly pigmented and can outshine almost all man-made colors. The approach chosen here was to keep to the green hues of the surroundings, but base the design on a muted range of unglazed ceramics – a distinctive but sympathetic palette. Smaller quantities of vitreous glass were added, both to enliven the color and give a variety of surface qualities. The glass is more reflective, catching the light and sparkling in sympathy with the water below.

The next challenge was to choose a style appropriate to the context. In a location dominated by living forms, it is important to decide whether to emulate the asymmetry of nature or to create a strong contrast by adopting a more stylized approach. Either treatment can succeed, but a compromise between the two risks producing an unsatisfactorily muddled result. In this case a formal and structured approach was adopted, taking individual elements of pond vegetation and making a row of strong images. Because it is a composition of different greens, some of the plant motifs almost disappear against their backgrounds but – because each panel works as a pattern as well as a representation – this adds to the subtlety of the overall piece. The strongest elements are the orange fish, standing out against the greens in the same way that the real goldfish swimming in the pond below glow out of the dark surrounding water.

The panel is edged by a row of rectangular pieces like a fringe on a carpet, but the motifs overlap the border and extend to the very edge. This creates the visual illusion that they are lying on top of the surrounding mosaic, echoing the way that the panel itself is suspended over the water.

This piece was made using the indirect method, which allowed a lot of experimentation with color combinations, rhythms of grout joints and patterns. It also meant that the sequence of individual panels could be altered to create a balanced finished effect. The piece was fixed to a hardwood framed exterior grade ply board with a very flexible proprietary adhesive (Bal-Flex) and grouted with a dark gray grout.

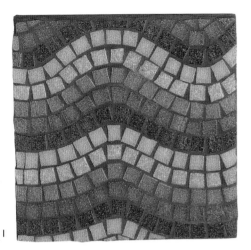

Water is a visually fascinating subject. Its combined qualities of reflectivity and transparency give it an almost endless variety of shifting appearances that can be expressed in a variety of techniques. As it is a subject that has been frequently depicted in mosaic, various conventions have arisen over time to symbolize seas and rivers.

WAVES AND COLOR

Because water is known to move in waves, laying mosaic in undulating lines immediately expresses wateriness as shown in the first example (left). Use of color is also a symbolic way to describe water: tones of blue and aqua not only present an accurate description of the Mediterranean sea but are also an agreed code for all water. Dark, stormy waters of muddy green and gray are more accurately depicted in the irregular undulations of example 2 (below).

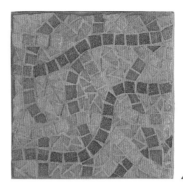

4

2

The long thin pieces emphasize the horizontal aspect of seascapes while the mix of colors and the small touches of mirror help to describe the shifting surface of the water, constantly changing and reflecting the light.

TRANSPARENCY

Example 3 (right) shows a traditional depiction of water found in Byzantine and medieval illustrations of Baptism. The shape of the figure is interrupted by alternate lines of blue mosaic carried, through from the surrounding water. It is a fascinating pictorial invention that illustrates the abstract and conceptual approach of early Christian art. It bears no relation to our experience of how a figure would look underwater, but its logic enables the viewer to read both figure and water simultaneously. Neither is submerged by the other.

SURFACE

Later traditions in art are more observational. Although very stylized, example 4 (above) shows the patterns created when three curving lines intersect, as in the formation of waves. It is a phenomenon observed by David Hockney and used in his paintings of Californian swimming pools. In mosaic, the curving lines are rendered in small squares while the surface between is expressed in randomly laid triangles so that the directions of movement are clearly shown against a lively but unified background.

3

POND SURROUND

The inspiration for this design came from the floor glass or "rust"mosaics of the early part of the twentieth century. Rust mosaic was a thick cube of vitreous material – reputedly made from recycled glass – and there are two opinions as to how it got its name. One is that it came from its maker – a British manufacturer called Mr Rust – the other is that it derived from the variation in color and irregularity of the material: a shortening of the Italian word "rustico".

One characteristic feature of a rust floor is its checkered border, which is often black and white, as here, but can be dark mauve or brown and white. Another characteristic, which this pond surround imitates, is a semi-random, closely jointed close-toned field color. (The "field"is the main part of a floor, describing everything within the border.) The original rust material has color variations within a single cube. Reproducing the effect is more difficult. Here the mosaic is cut from a mixture of Mexican and Italian glass. It was necessary to use Mexican material to imitate the range of sizes of the original, but the Italian glass helped to broaden the available range of color and tone. So, although it might not be immediately obvious to the eye, there are three whites and four blacks used in the border, giving the mosaic an authentically flickery appearance. (The field was cut from three colors of Mexican glass.)

The pond was dug a couple of years before the mosaic was made and the pond liner extended into the earth around it. This made it impossible to dig foundations for a screed on which the mosaic could be laid: digging might pierce the liner and endanger the pond. Any mosaic would have to be sturdy and supply its own foundations. The only solution was to cast the pond surround as a series of paving slabs.

Whatever size the slabs were to be, they needed to be a repeatable module on both the long and the short sides of the pond. Having arrived at a size that worked, a casting frame was made. As the mosaic was made on paper and the slab cast over it (see "Casting"on page 120 for further practical information) the same frame could be reused for all of them. The four corners were made by putting a couple of pieces of timber across the width of the long frame to form a square at each end. This made it easy to make two corners at a time. The only remaining issue was whether or not it looked more effective to double up the checkered border between cast slabs. In the end, both options were used. The unpredictability seemed to work with the rustic mosaic.

FOUNTAIN

This piece was inspired by the gently trickling wall fountains seen in the streets of Rome. The starting point for the design was the color of the container that holds the water pump and acts as a reservoir. The feed pipe emerges from a drain hole, sealed against leaks with building silicone. The wall behind the fountain is decorated with a textural mosaic whose design suggests its function.

The container is glazed blue, with a brown and black ceramic body, which influenced the choice of colors in the mosaic, as did the red-brown brick wall against which the fountain was to stand. (Make sure you have bought your container before producing a design, or you run the risk of having to design the mosaic twice.)

The design is divided into horizontal bands, rather like layers of rock or soil. The vertical lines of foil-backed glass that cut across the horizontal bands are reminiscent of the fall of water even when the fountain is not in play. The design is deliberately asymmetrical and irregular, although there are rules governing the irregularity: for example, the way the four vertical lines change color consistently as they descend through the background strata. Three of them are made from reflective metallic backed glass – copper, silver, gold and bronze – the other from marble and smalti. Four identical vertical lines are repeated at the side. A single line of riven marble contrasts with the glass.

Both the marble and the smalti are thicker than the glass, and stand slightly proud of the plane of most of the mosaic. This gives an interesting textural contrast, and acts as a visual counterbalance to the recessive qualities of the foil-backed glass. In other words, if the silver and gold seem to go back from the surface, they are balanced by the smalti and marble that appear to come forward.

As you can see, the vitreous glass is laid without regard to the lines of coursing. Random shapes and sizes are used; the colors are not entirely random, as they tend to be of a similar tone. The only exception to this tonal rule is where white has been used, splashed throughout the mosaic to suggest water. This method of laying mosaic was very popular in the 1960s and is a good way of escaping the tyranny of the andamenti (the lines in which mosaic may be laid). It can be especially useful for a beginner.

54

Mosaics are an unusual art form in that when fixed in situ they become an integral part of their location. This close relationship between the site and the mosaic can be expressed in the content of the mosaic itself. Illustrated is a mosaic pavement based on an aerial view of the part of the country in which the garden is situated. It seemed an appropriate idea as the site is near an American air base and low-flying jets are a regular feature of life. The aerial perspective of the countryside with its patchwork of fields and gardens is itself a mosaic of interlocking shapes, and it was an attractive idea to try to interpret it in that medium.

LOCATION

Another way of making something specific to a particular place is to use found materials. The piece illustrated (left) is a light-box with a collection of sea-washed glass fragments stuck to a clear glass plate and illuminated from behind. It is called the "Lower Hope", named after a stretch of beach along the Thames Estuary that was rich in old glass and china fragments. The pale, washed-out colors of the glass are curiously reminiscent of the watery light over the river; the weathered fragments bring back memories of a time when this was the busiest shipping lane in the world. A map mounted at the back of the box shows the location of the beach and the snaking path of the river.

As the air base (left) is close to the sea, the coastline makes a strong identifying feature. The sea is expressed in parallel lines of blue ceramic with tiny strips of mirror interspersed that catch the light and twinkle like waves in the sun. The rivers and creeks are also made of fractured mirror while the cars along the main roads are formed of tiny pieces of colored glass mosaic. The location of the mosaic itself is marked with a gold piece and the pavement gives viewers a broader sense of their surroundings and an unusual sense of place.

CHAPTER 4
WALL MOSAICS

Exterior walls can be attractive, both supporting plants and giving shade and structure to a garden or terrace. However, they can also be blank areas, dry and dark, against which nothing will thrive. Mosaic can work well on walls like these, bringing color and life to difficult areas. For obvious practical reasons it is far easier to use textured and uneven materials on walls than it is on the floor. This means that you have much more freedom to use tesserae for their textural properties. An example of this is the large striped marble and smalti panel discussed on pages 70–71.

This wall panel (left) from Khirbat al-Mafjar takes the natural world as its theme, and creates something which would be appealing whatever the season. The subject matter works well in the context of a garden, and the subtle handling of naturalistic color is inspiring. All the elements of the design have a delicate balance – something the wall panel of Icarus falling to earth (pages 66–9) also manages to achieve. Moreover, this panel makes imaginative use of mirror tiles. It is not uncommon today to see entire walls made from mirror mosaic which, when laid in a slightly uneven way, throws light in many different directions, helping to create an illusion of greater depth.

COLOR WALL

Many of us will have a window that overlooks an unsightly exterior wall. By their very nature, walls of this kind are likely to be shaded and north facing, which of course makes it difficult to grow anything to disguise or soften them. Places like these are perfect for mosaic.

This wall is overlooked from a kitchen and a dining-room and was a depressing sight from both. The wall was so close to the kitchen window that it had to be treated as part of the room, which brought its own problems. The colors used had to have a sympathetic relationship with the decorative scheme of kitchen and dining room but allow for the fact that, while the interior color scheme was likely to change, the mosaic would be a long-lasting feature. The palette needed to be broad enough not to constrain the client's choices inside the house.

The mosaic is made in quarter-cut vitreous glass. The design is based on lines and rectangles, the lines running through from section to section. This makes the design relatively easy to make, but helps to calm down the busy effect of a wide palette of color. Throughout this book we discuss the importance of constraint, of making rules in order to discover creative ways of breaking them.

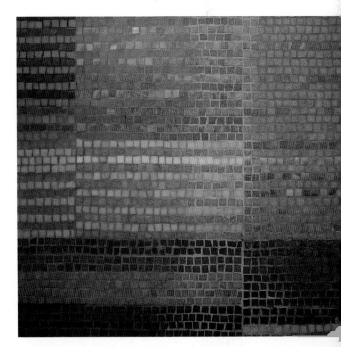

This design illustrates the principle. The upper half of the mosaic establishes a rule: boxes of colored lines divided into darker and lighter tones. The box on the far right is different: it breaks the rule that the eye has come to expect and surprises us. No rule, no surprise.

One of the enjoyable things color can do is to create a feeling of warmth. The patch of light tones combined with bright colors (the swathe across the middle with yellow and green stripes) gives an illusory feeling that light is falling on the mosaic. This works even though the brightly colored lines above are from an entirely different part of the palette. The effect is produced by the background color being a consistently lighter version of the one used as a background to the darker area above. It gives the mosaic a glowing effect.

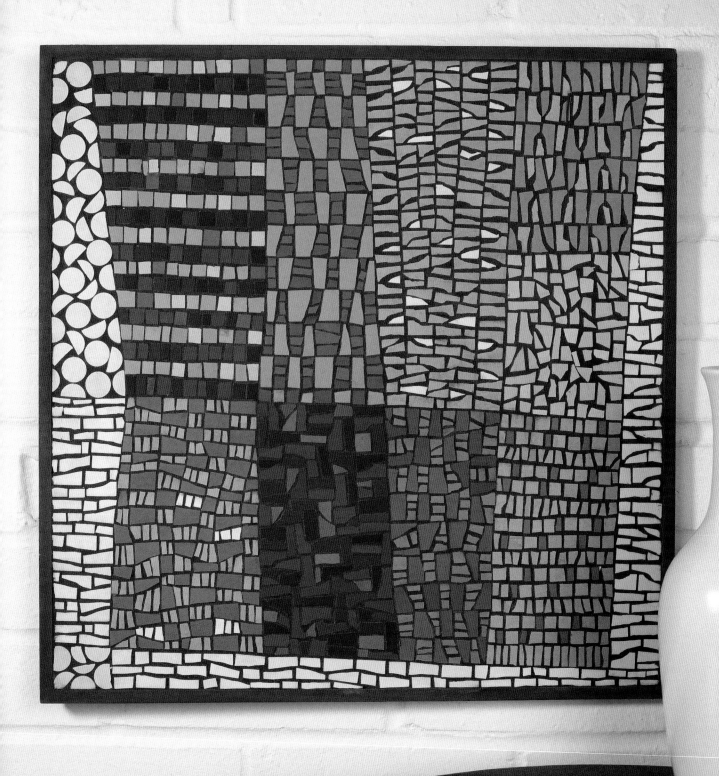

CERAMIC MOSAIC PANEL

This panel is made from odds and ends of ceramic found in the Workshop. The project was an attempt to demonstrate the principal that it is not so much how you cut tiles that matters, as how you lay them. The peculiar and unconventional cuts here are given a rhythm by keeping an even gap between them. The design is intended to be a series of experiments with different techniques, rather like a sampler in needlework.

The piece is made by the reverse method, probably the most useful of all mosaic methods because it allows you to make projects somewhere other than the place you wish to fix them. It also allows you to correct mistakes: all you need to do is wet the backing paper and the glue will release the tiles. If in the process you accidentally pierce the paper, it can be patched with another small piece.

FOUND OBJECTS PANEL

The interest of this piece comes from the combination of objects and materials that have very different qualities, an approach that can be difficult to control. Mosaics made of mixed-media often have a careless exuberance, but little sense of structure. Often the impulse to make something out of found objects is the desire to use up collections of oddments languishing in jam jars. It is almost inevitable, therefore, that you will have unequal quantities of your treasures and that combining them in any rational way will be difficult. By using materials in a more disciplined way, the individual elements are easier to see and have greater impact.

The solution presented by this panel was to use a lot of a single material – the pebbles – with the found objects running across in horizontal bands, like strata in rock formations. A further device for unifying the materials was to divide the panel into black and white vertical stripes crossed by bands of color. Read horizontally, the bands cohere because they are made of the same material (as in the band of buttons) or materials with similar qualities. The glass marbles, little plastic beads and metal nuts have a relationship with the black and white pebbles because they are the same sort of shape and size.

In the vertical direction the bands unite because the materials are organized into black and white stripes. Again this rule is interpreted rather loosely; the buttons and marble cubes are black and white but most of the materials are dark and light. One vertical band uses the strong colors of beads and buttons, the transparency of clear marbles and the complexity of fragments of blue and white china. Because the overall structure of the piece is so strong and ordered these outbreaks of flamboyance are lively but not too chaotic.

Using such unevenly shaped objects the adhesive bed will inevitably be visible in the finished piece. White adhesive was used for the pale and transparent colors, and gray for the darker ones. This helps to emphasize the light and dark bands and, because the shapes are defined by simple straight lines, it is easy to apply the different colors. It is easiest to work with both simultaneously so that you can lay the horizontal bands and be sure that they will line through. The panel is designed to hang outdoors and all the materials are reasonably weatherproof (remember to make sure that any metal components are stainless steel or aluminum or else they will rust and stain the surrounding materials). The backing is a mineral-fiber board set into a hardwood frame and the adhesive is an exterior cement-based adhesive. It would not be feasible or desirable to grout such an uneven piece, and some of the old glazed china might suffer in severe weather. It would therefore be advisable to take such a panel indoors during the winter months.

CHARYBDIS

This framed wall panel portrays the mythical subject of Charybdis, a daughter of Poseidon who was banished to live in a sea cave. Furious at her fate, she would watch for passing ships then suck up the ocean creating the deadly whirlpool that almost engulfed Odysseus.

The main difficulty in making a piece of this kind is the extreme difference between how it looks close to and how it looks from a distance. When working on it, you will easily be able to assess the successful juxtaposition of different materials and the harmony of the colors. However, the overall impression when viewed from a distance will be quite different: the form of the face and the nuances of expression will carry great importance.

The best way to ensure a successful outcome is to work from a drawing. Trace the drawing onto the supporting panel and place the original drawing on another movable board. The materials can then be laid out dry on top of the drawing, which can be carefully lowered to the floor to give

you a greater viewing distance. This can be further increased by standing on a chair. It is quite remarkable how such a composite image transforms as you get further away from it. This is of course the principal behind the "dots" of newspaper photographs, but it works just as well with much larger individual units. When you are happy with your arrangement, which may involve much getting up and down from the chair – a useful slimming exercise! – you can transfer them to the final piece.

Covering a small area of the drawing/panel at a time with a cement-based adhesive bed you can move pieces across one by one and rebuild the picture. (A gray adhesive is used, which breaks up the light and dark areas equally and unifies the whole.) You must try to notice where your adjustments vary from the drawing below in order to place the pieces in the right relationship in the adhesive bed. This is more difficult than it sounds because it is easy to get confused and lose registration points as the one drawing is covered with adhesive and the other, with the image of loose pieces, is gradually demolished. However if you use a slow-setting adhesive you will have plenty of time to make further adjustments to the final piece when you have again looked at it from a distance and worked out if changes need to be made.

The materials for this project were selected partly because they are largely natural and sea-like, but also because of their harmonious color range. Even the transparent marbles have a greenish hue that complements the greens of the pebbles and shells. Contrast is provided by the careful use of black and white pebbles that emphasize the face and define the shape of the head. The yellow and black shells lend a hint of color to the cheeks and relate to the richer colors of the glass beads used for the lips. The eyes are made up of sea-washed glass fragments with pupils of old cats-eye marbles. This gives the image a glassy and rather fierce stare: a subtle reminder of Charybdis' monstrous powers. As with the Found Objects Panel on the previous pages, it is recommended to take this panel indoors over winter.

ICARUS

This piece was designed for the roof garden of an urban penthouse. The location is very dramatic: high above the surrounding buildings with the vast expanse of un-interrupted sky as the dominating feature of the terrace. The mosaic was to be positioned on a triangular gable wall and so the panel was designed as an arc of a circle to complement the shape of the wall. The subject chosen is based on the Greek story of Icarus who flew too close to the sun with wings of wax and feathers. The wax melted and Icarus fell helplessly through the air back to earth. In the design, he is shown in his head-long descent surrounded by the feathers of his broken wings.

The materials used in the roof garden are natural timbers and muted color-washed walls, and the general style is imaginative and contemporary. It seemed appropriate, therefore, to use a limited range of unglazed ceramic colors that would not be too strident against their surroundings.

Having made these fundamental decisions about shape, material and subject matter the design had to be worked out in detail. The composition of the piece is generated by the unusual shape of the panel. To exploit this as a positive feature the figure is arranged in relation to the frame with the ends of all his limbs equidistant from the edges and the framework of his wings radiating out from the figure to the circumference.

The most critical aspect of the design is the selection of the color range. It is essential to the meaning of the piece that it should feel light and airy so that the figure has a sense of weightless falling. Pale colors of very similar tone were therefore chosen, but this can create problems of clarity as the colors can blend into each other, losing definition and outline. The pale yellow and cream are paler than the green background, while the gray is slightly darker and these have therefore been used wherever clarity of definition was important. Occasionally the pale blue does abut the pale green as on the arms and right foot, and these small areas of indistinct but delicate tonal juxtaposition contribute to the overall lightness of feel. Similarly a true white has been used in the feathers because the relative brightness brings them forward and creates the illusion of floating in front of the figure. The mirror tiles used to represent the metal spokes will be unpredictable, changing under different times and conditions, but their essential reflectivity and sparkle will never be as heavy as a continuous line of color.

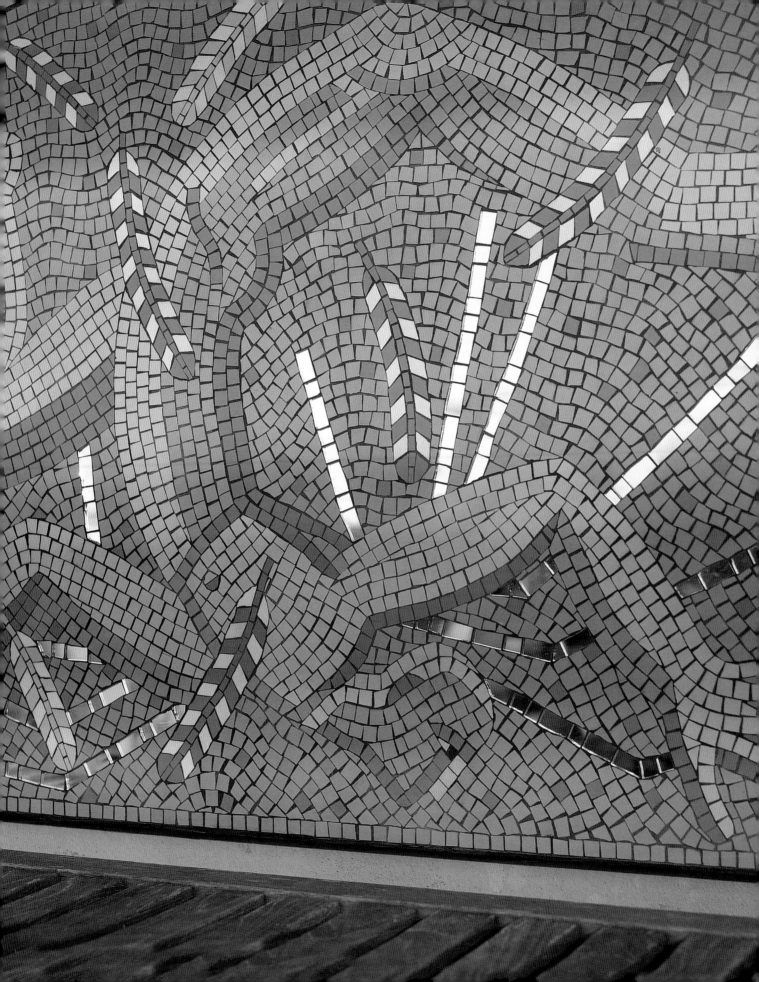

These issues of composition and color balance can be worked out in advance on a drawing using colored pencils or pastels. This does not have to be a carefully finished object as it is a part of the process rather than an end in itself. The mosaic will be based on the drawing, but not a slavish copy of it because as you work you need to have the freedom to make adjustments and improvements suggested by the medium.

In this piece there are various areas in which the translation into mosaic has created complexity and interest that was not apparent on the drawing. In the figure itself, the direction of laying is of great importance in the description of form. Junctions between different directions can create unintentional lines without any reference to human anatomy so they must be carefully positioned, preferably at a color change whose outline will make sense in the context of the overall design. Along the arms you will notice that care has been taken at the elbows, particularly in the cream color, to let the lines of laying merge without cutting and thus avoiding a peculiar seam across the arm. Curved lines of laying can also create the illusion of three-dimensional form in a similar way to contour lines on a relief map. For example, the left knee-cap has been laid in concentric lines to indicate that it occupies a different plane from

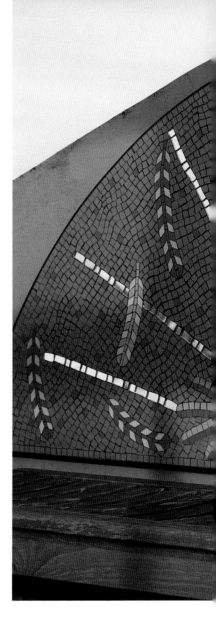

the thigh and calf. Changes of direction can also help describe form, as where the direction of laying across the chest emphasizes the twist in the body as the left shoulder turns back above the head.

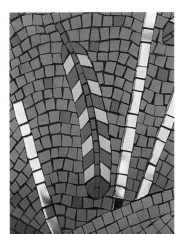

The treatment of the feathers, using shapes cut from larger pieces, gives them a simplicity and boldness that helps them to stand out. The larger scale makes them appear closer to the surface and clearly in front of the figure and background. Similarly, the long rectangular shapes of the mirrors making up the framework of the wings stands out against the even squares of the background and emphasizes the linearity of the spokes.

The background is given interest by being laid to an unevenly undulating line that is generated by the irregularity of hand-cut pieces. This technique allows you to be very relaxed about cutting and to use up rejected quarters from other jobs. However, you do have to concentrate

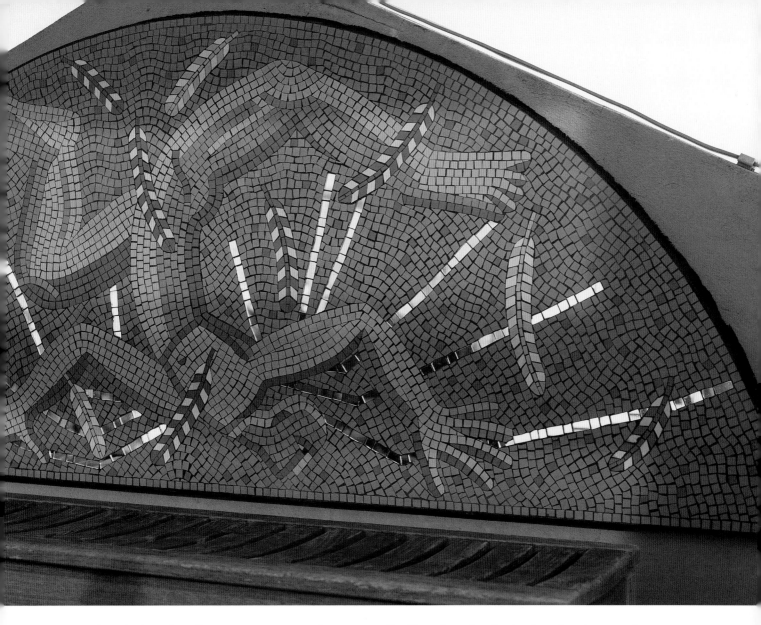

when laying the tiles to create a consistent overall effect, insuring both that the degree of unevenness in the line is constant throughout and also that the lines follow through either side of interruption so that the basic idea of following the circumference is clearly readable. Occasional pieces of gray have been dotted into the background to give a flickering effect which echoes the more dramatic flicker of the reflections in the mirrors.

Although designed for a specific site, this panel has been made so that it can be moved if necessary. Rather than fixing directly to the rendered surface it has been made in a timber frame fixed with secret fixings to the wall behind. The panel has an exterior-grade plywood backing board and a narrow hardwood frame. To reduce the possibility of the whole panel warping, the back of the board was protected from moisture penetration with an exterior varnish and was fixed back at five points, three along the bottom and two around the circumference. The mosaic itself was made using the indirect method and fixed to the board with a highly flexible adhesive.

TEXTURE PANEL

This panel was designed for the same garden as the Color Wall (pages 58-9). As there was a deliberate contrast in materials between the two pieces, it seemed a good idea to keep a similar design theme: that of stripes. The Texture Panel is made from riven marble and smalti. The marble is muted in color and the smalti more intense. It isn't normally sensible to leave mosaic ungrouted outdoors because of the danger of rainwater running between the joints of the tiles, freezing and expanding, forcing the tiles off the panel. However, this panel could be left ungrouted thanks to an excellent new rubberized adhesive now on the British market called Bal-Flex. (Similar flexible adhesives are produced under a variety of brand names in other countries.) This adhesive allows a certain amount of movement to take place without the tiles coming away from the substrate. The back and sides of the board were sealed with a compatible sealant, but the face of the board was left unprimed. Adhesive manufacturers vary in their recommended practice: make sure you follow their instructions carefully. When making a project of this type, it is essential to find a manufacturer who will guarantee its products outdoors on wood.

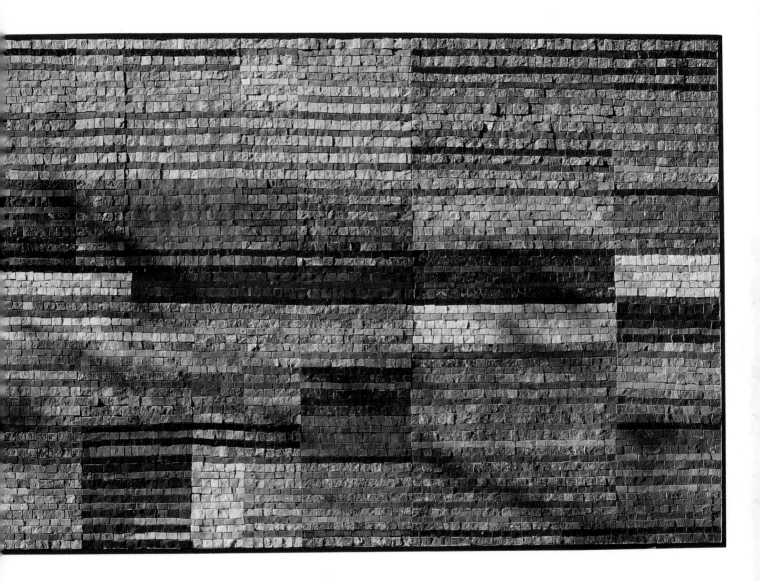

Although it would have been possible to make this piece by the indirect method, it was in fact made by working directly onto the board. The choice was made because of the riven nature of the material. Smalti, although uneven, is color consistent throughout. The marble, however, can look strikingly different in color once the material body has been cut open. Using the indirect method would mean working with the riven face hidden, giving an inaccurate idea of the balance of colors in the finished piece.

CHAPTER 5
OBJECTS AND SCULPTURES

The sole purpose of sculptures is to delight the eye. Being three-dimensional objects that need to be seen in the round, they can also take up a fair amount of space and unless you live in a palace it can be difficult to accommodate them inside the home. Outside, however, there may be more opportunity to indulge a taste for the purely decorative .

Statuary in a garden setting is an important tradition in garden design associated both with the great Renaissance gardens in Italy and the less formal English gardens of the eighteenth century. It was used to provide points of focus around which the planting was planned and, because of its often figurative subject matter, it could introduce a sense of scale against which to measure the grandeur of nature. Slightly smaller than life-size figures were sometimes used to help exaggerate a sense of distance and therefore the perceived size of the garden itself. In the smaller domestic garden, sculpture can still be used to punctuate a space, encouraging the eye to experience a series of impressions rather than taking in the whole space in one glance. The human figure can be a good vertical form in the context of trees and tall bushes and non-representational but organic forms can also be very successful. Animals always look at home in a natural setting and sculptures are better behaved than real livestock.

The idea of covering sculptures with mosaic has ancient roots. The Aztecs used fragments of turquoise combined with rock crystal and mother of pearl to cover human skulls and masks.

There was renewed interest in the twentieth century as shown in the sculptural forms of the Parc Guell by Josep Maria Jujol in Barcelona and the enormous figures of Niki de Saint Phalle's Tarot Garden in Tuscany. A more continuous tradition is to be found in "outsider art", that is the works of people outside the conventional art world who are motivated by the need to make things rather than the desire to be known as artists. A surprisingly high proportion of these works is covered in mosaic, usually broken china and tiles but sometimes bottles, bangles and buttons. These "found" materials allow the usually poverty-stricken artists to introduce color and pattern into their work in an economical way. It is also possible that the rather time-consuming and laborious properties of fashioning mosaic appeal to these obsessive workers as they assemble fragments of discarded rubbish into orderly, if sometimes incomprehensible, private worlds. One of the most impressive examples is the Rock Garden in Chandigarh. This was built by Nek Chand, a local road inspector who began collecting debris in the course of his work which he then used to decorate clay figures that he made in a small clearing in the jungle (see picture opposite). Gradually his scavenging extended to all the domestic waste tips in the area and the garden began to grow with ranks of figures and animals marching in purposeful formation, unseen by anyone else in the world. Eventually it was discovered by a jungle-clearing party and reported to the authorities who made the surprisingly enlightened decision not only to preserve the garden but also to pay Chand a salary and provide him with a workforce so that his project could continue.

If you feel that garden sculpture is too ambitious or ostentatious, you can also use mosaic to decorate functional garden objects such as planters and flower-pots. Garden centers provide a wide range of suitable bases made of terracotta and concrete that are both strong and weather-proof. Avoid plastic bases as these are too flexible and try to choose simple shapes that will not present complicated surfaces to cover in mosaic. Builders' merchants can also be a useful source of suitable bases such as chimney pots and drainage pipes that can be used as decorative columns and plant stands.

GLASS MOSAIC PLANTER

The careful use of mosaic is an excellent way of introducing color into a garden, particularly in the winter months but also at those other odd times of year when all your plants have given up flowering simultaneously. Planters are particularly useful in this way, as they can be moved around to add interest where it is needed most. It can, however, be difficult to make strong colors look sympathetic in an outdoor setting as they will be in the context of the complex and predominantly more muted tones of nature. One way of looking at this is to examine the way in which bright colors generally appear in the natural environment. The eye-catching intensity of bright flowers, berries or insects is enhanced by their relative smallness against large areas of less intense color, and brightness can be used to great effect as highlights in a more subdued color field. This is the simple idea behind the design of this planter, where a range of bright yellows, oranges and pinks are used sparingly against grays and murky blues and greens. The colors do not repeat around the pot, so different effects are achieved on different sides. This is useful because you can turn the pot around according to what is planted in it or where it is positioned in the garden.

Color is not the only consideration in designing planters. Shape is very important, both in relation to the plant above and the general surroundings. The tall cylindrical shape chosen here would suit tall, upright plants such as grasses or lilies and its simple lines complement a modern urban patio or decked yard. The shape also influences the mosaic treatment; the proportions of the pot are echoed in the rectangular glass mosaics that are sometimes laid vertically in harmony with the form of the pot and sometimes horizontally to create a contrast. The parallel sides of the pot provide an opportunity to execute a simple design of vertical stripes which would not be easy to achieve on a traditionally shaped flowerpot. Planters with a curved or tapering profile lend themselves to horizontal stripes only.

The pot has been made using the direct method. The fixing materials and mosaic materials are all frost proof, but terracotta pots may crack in extreme cold and should be protected or taken indoors in winter.

MOSAIC HEAD

This piece was inspired by the sculptures of the classical world, and its form and expression refer to the stern and commanding effigies of goddesses such as Diana and Athena. The use of mosaic is also a classical allusion since it was widely used on walls and pavements in the Greek and Roman empires and this work therefore fuses two ancient traditions into an object that is both familiar and unlikely. The head is life-sized and needs to be viewed at eye-level. It could occupy the top of a gatepost or column or perhaps stand in a bricked-up opening or niche.

In making a piece such as this the final covering of mosaic is only one part of the challenge. Creating a suitable sub-base is equally important and in this case there were three stages: a clay head was covered by a mold from which a plaster cast was formed. (See pages 124–5 for full instructions.) When you come to cover the head in mosaic, you will transform it from a rounded piece to a surface made up of hundreds of faceted planes. This in itself is of strong visual interest so everything else can be kept very simple. There is no need to employ different tones to describe the form as the falling of the light will do that itself. Subtle variations in light and shadow are more visible on non-reflecting surfaces that do not have the distractions of glinting highlights. For these reasons a single color of unglazed ceramic was chosen to describe the skin color, with very similar shades for the hair and necklace.

In a restricted color scheme the lines of laying are very noticeable and must be designed with care. Junctions between different directions will create strong lines and should be avoided except where they occur at clear changes in plane, such as at the nose and ears. For the face, the lines of the eyebrows and eye sockets have been followed, generating gently curved lines which express the rounded form. The neck and shoulders follow the line of the necklace, while the hair runs out from the center parting except around the roll at the back where the pieces are laid diagonally to give the impression of a twisted lock of hair. Before beginning, mark out

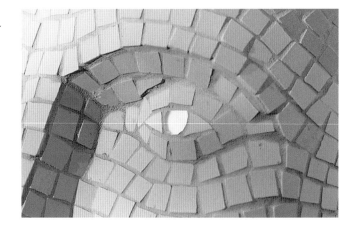

the joint lines in pencil so that you can anticipate tricky junctions in advance. Where the different directions meet, for instance beside the eyes and between the cheeks and the neck, you may find that you need to lose a line or two to make the lines flow through. This is best done by reducing two rows into a single larger piece which then starts a new line without resorting to tapering triangles, which can look clumsy.

In any face the eyes are the most important element and it is a good idea to start with them, both because they give expression and character and because they set up the lines of laying. In this piece, where all the colors are very muted, the eyes are also understated by using frosted mirror for the pupils. In color this is very similar to both the white of the eyes and the off-white of the skin but the slight translucence of the material gives it a depth and a gleam which adds a glimmer of life to the otherwise ghostly face. (A dark face can be just as arresting, as seen above.)

MYTHICAL ANIMAL

This large piece would enliven the corner of any spacious garden. As well as having a strong sculptural form generated by the idea of a large animal sitting on all fours, the broad back provides a useful seat for small children.

Mythical beasts appear in the stories of many cultures and are often combinations of familiar animals, for example the griffin which is half lion and half eagle, and the chimera which is lion, goat and snake combined. There is something attractive in making up a new creature, but it is almost impossible not to make references to pre-existing animals. This piece has turned out as a winged dog and while it lacks the heroic qualities of some mythical beasts it would make a good guardian beside a doorway, welcoming visitors and patiently awaiting every home-coming. Its simple shape and stylized decoration recall ancient Egyptian and Assyrian sculptures and reliefs where sculptural forms were often decorated with inscribed patterns. Here the wings and fur are described with linear patterns and the legs are simply "drawn" onto the three-dimensional surface.

As with the mosaic head, a major part of the project is the making of the base. The technique is similar but because of the scale of the piece it would not be very practical to make a full-sized clay version. Instead a clay model was made in order to work out the basic shape and the dimensions were worked out from this. (See page 125 for full instructions.)

Before applying mosaic to the base, it is a good idea to do some colored drawings to work out how you are going to proceed. They will help you to select appropriate colors and patterns. Bear in mind that objects in a garden setting will be surrounded by different textures and patterns to which the design should respond and relate. There may also be great contrast in the garden between light and shade, so the design needs to be bold enough to read against these distractions. On the winged dog the legs and wings are described in strong dark lines and the patterns and markings are drawn at a large scale to help them stand out. In contrast to these emphatic graphic elements, the color range is restricted to four different greens and a black so that the overall effect is restrained and unfussy.

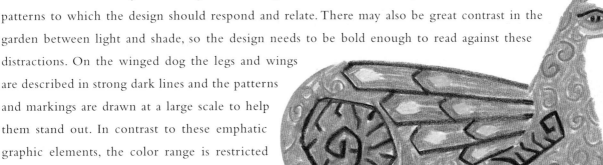

Having decided on the design, you can then draw the main lines onto the cement shell with pencil or charcoal. The two sides do not have to be perfectly symmetrical as they will not be seen simultaneously, but you need to be careful with the symmetry of the head or else it may look lop-sided when viewed from the front. Pay attention to the angle of the eyebrows and the eyes as this will have an impact on the animal's expression. Here, the eyes have been made with "reverse" gold, that is gold used with the green face showing, so that they blend in with the rest of the colors but have a distinctive and lively glitter. The ears have been carefully covered to avoid using any small pieces, which would be particularly vulnerable in such an exposed position.

A diagonal direction of laying was used on the wings to suggest the barbs of feathers, while the legs were unified as distinct areas by laying the background to run parallel to the barred markings. The rest of the body is decorated with curls and stripes which are outlined in the background color and the spaces between are filled with a consistent but non-directional mixture of half and whole tiles. This system allows even the strangest shape to be covered without resort to small pieces that look ugly and are difficult to lay.

When someone starts to collect something – from seed packets to train timetables – it is generally because the item is either interesting or useful. Both categories work well as starting points for visual treatments. Look at what you collect, or what interests you, analyze its appeal and attempt to express it in your work. This can be a good starting point for experimenting with design.

These cotton reels demonstrate the appeal of repetition. Their identical shape and size allows you to concentrate on the elements of tone and color. The way the darker shades and lighter tones fuse together makes the intensity of the yellows particularly striking. By loose-laying mosaic tiles in formal arrangements like this, you can learn just how intense some of the colors can be. You may be surprised at how recessive some apparently bright colors become in combination with others of a similar tone. A further appeal of this collection is the way in which the individual reels are shaded across a single color. You can use this effect in mosaic to create a sense of form.

You might draw a mistaken conclusion from looking at these boxes of buttons. There is a controlling structure here – the segmented system of the boxes – that allows the collections of buttons of a single color across a tonal range to be read clearly. Tonal variation within a single area of the spectrum can be visually confusing, and difficult to read. You need clues to help you. This demonstrates a universal principal of effective design: if you want complexity in one area you need simplicity in another.

This collection of marbles shows another couple of issues you may encounter when designing in mosaic. You can see how reflective they are, so much so in the case of the glassy ones that their forms become quite difficult to read. The most reflective materials are obviously mirror glass, vitreous glass and smalti, although it can also sometimes be an issue with marble. Think about the vantage points from which your work can be seen, and consider the degrees of light and shade both of the mosaic and the viewpoint. You will also notice that the combination of large and small marbles has a different effect from a collection of single-sized marbles. Surprises in scale can add drama to a design.

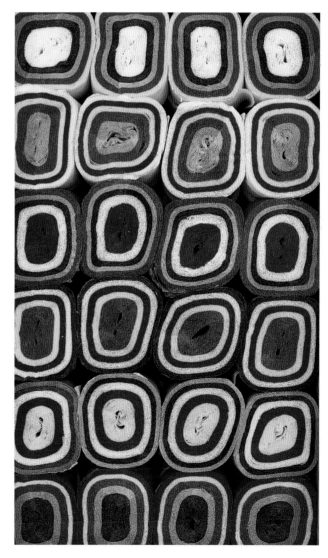

This collection of paper streamers is based on the simple idea of a repeated form. Repetition is in the nature of mosaic. This can range from the micro – the repeated shape of a tile – through the modular – patterns made by an arrangement of tiles – to the macro, in which repetition is the subject matter of the design. When a visual idea is repeated, small differences can take on an expressive richness. Here, the streamers are mostly arranged vertically, so where one is slightly squashed or has been arranged horizontally, the variation becomes exciting. Saturated color and contrast help to give the streamers visual impact.

COLLECTIONS

CHAPTER 6
CONSERVATORIES AND PORCHES

Mosaic floors with their durable surface and decorative potential, make an excellent transition from indoors to outdoors. They can add an individual touch to entrances and provide an introduction to the character and function of a building. The Roman port of Ostia Antica was famous for its black and white mosaics, and in the forum they depicted the symbols of the crafts and businesses that occupied the shops. Illustrated opposite is an entrance mosaic found in many Roman towns: the familiar *Cave Canem* or "Beware of the Dog".

In the nineteenth and twentieth centuries, mosaic continued to be used at the entrances to shops, bars and other public buildings. Sometimes these were very simple, single-color mosaics with plain string borders; occasionally the field is laid in a "fan" pattern that lends an elegant decorative flourish. An example of nineteenth-century fan flooring is to be found at London's National Portrait Gallery where the impressive entrance mosaic leads on to further areas of mosaic fan inside the building. Most examples, however, are on a much more modest scale but even the smallest mosaic doorstep will add a certain charm to a building. Many mosaics of this period display a high level of craftsmanship that definitely repays a closer look. Mosaic work throughout Europe remained the preserve of the expatriate Italian communities so one can safely assume that the careful technique displayed in many nineteenth- and twentieth-century commercial and domestic works is the product of centuries of experience handed down through the mosaicists' families.

Mosaic porches present an opportunity for names and numbers and for other signs relevant to the public face of a building. Conservatories, by contrast, are usually at the back of a building and represent the more private and personal aspect of the home. The mosaic shown below is the floor of a cactus house that the clients had built to house their collection of exotic plants. Conservatories – as the traditional space between the house and the garden – often combine features of both inside and outside. Plants co-habit happily with soft furnishings, and garden tools hang next to mirrors and pictures. Mosaic panels can reflect this attractive ambiguity, treating subjects inspired by plants and gardens in a decorative style that relates to carpets and domestic fabrics. Glass walls also represent a good opportunity to hang translucent mosaic panels to good effect.

Porches are a very practical location for mosaic pavements as they provide shelter from the worst of the elements and some easing of winter temperatures due to their proximity to the heated home. Conservatories, while showing these advantages, can also present quite difficult technical challenges. This is because of the extreme contrast between the high summer temperatures created by the sunlight and the low winter temperatures caused by the dramatic heat loss though glass. All this causes expansion and contraction in mosaic backing materials that can lead to cracking or even failure of the adhesive bond, so special care should be taken to use flexible fixing materials. For larger mosaics, whether they be tabletops or pavements, it is wise to allow for a silicone mastic joint around the perimeter to prevent undue stress from building up on the edge of the tiles.

TRANSLUCENT PANEL

One of the most attractive properties of glass is its translucence. The intensity of color created by light shining through colored glass is far greater than colors created by reflected light from opaque surfaces. This is an effect that is familiar from stained glass windows in churches where the windows glow out of the surrounding darkness. Similar effects can be achieved with mosaic by fixing translucent glass to clear glass panels that can then be placed in front of a light source or window to allow daylight to shine through. Conservatories are an ideal location with their large expanses of glass and as an extra bonus you will find that direct sunlight will cast colored shadows onto the floor or opposite wall.

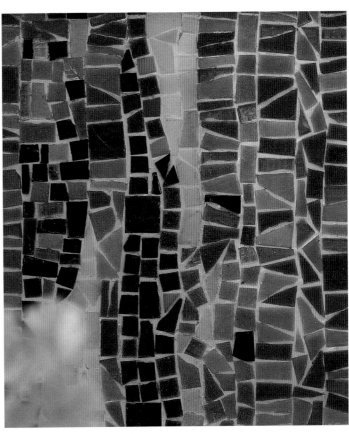

When embarking on a translucent piece you must select your mosaic materials with care. Some vitreous glass colors are translucent but others are not. A lot of the bright colors such as orange and red are disappointingly dull when held up to the light, while others may change color altogether when light shines through them: a dark charcoal gray, for instance, can become a beautiful dark green. Another pitfall is that the translucence depends on the chemical composition and firing of the tiles and this can vary from batch to batch. Consequently within a single color, tiles that look identical on the surface may be completely different when held up to the light: one being dazzlingly translucent the other completely opaque. A different option is to use stained glass, which can be cut into small pieces with a glass cutter. This technique allows you to use a wider variety of shapes and sizes, but stained glass comes in a limited range of colors and it tends to be rather expensive.

This little panel shows how a very simple arrangement, grouping different shades of vitreous glass into blocks of color, can create a lively and interesting effect. Because this piece is grouted with a clear silicone the joints stand out very brightly against the colored tiles and it is this tracery of pattern overlaying the color blocks that animates the panel. The occasional use of opaque tiles gives extra contrast and drama to the piece.

The indirect method was chosen for this piece but you can to use the direct method, spreading a thin layer of clear silicone on the glass before sticking the pieces into it. However, silicone can be quite messy to use and is difficult to remove if it gets in the wrong place. A further problem is that it hardens quickly when exposed to air leaving you a limited "open" time in which to work. One advantage of the direct method is that you have the option of grouting with a conventional dark grout. This will, of course, be opaque and will give the finished piece a tracery of black joints and an appearance more like a stained glass window. If you choose to employ this method, you must be careful when fixing to insure that the silicone does not come up through the joints, as this will prevent the grout from filling the gaps and be very obvious when held up to the light. The small wooden frame that surrounds this panel enables it to be hung in a window where it can catch the light.

NUMBER PANEL

Making a house number to hang beside the front door is a popular mosaic project, and this large piece illustrates a wide variety of possible materials and effects. It forms a decorative panel in itself but could also provide inspiration for smaller projects made from your own collections of found objects. The intention is that the panel should be hung in a porch or conservatory where it would be protected from the weather, and this allows a surprising range of materials to be used.

Quite apart from any functional purpose, numbers and letters are effective design elements in purely visual terms, using a limited language of lines and curves to form shapes that relate to each other and form pleasing combinations. They have evolved to be easy to write and this gives them a simplicity and elegance that is also easy on the eye. (See "Lettering" on pages 30–31.) They are also the most powerful symbols in our culture, capable of carrying meanings on many different levels. The number of your own house will carry a personal meaning for you, while some numbers convey a much wider message, such as "1984" with its connotations of totalitarian oppression.

One of the purposes of this panel is to demonstrate that you can make a mosaic out of anything that comes in small units or that can be cut or broken into small pieces. Within this overall principle, however, it is important to set yourself some constraints or else the finished piece will have no cohesion. You are aiming to create a piece that is full of richness and visual interest; you do not want it to look like a display at a garage sale. Select materials that have some quality in common with their neighbors – whether it be shape or thickness or color – and this will help to create a sense of order. In this panel there is one property shared by all the materials used and that is "hardness": they are all made of rigid metal, glass or plastic and have generally been acquired at hardware stores. It would be equally effective to make a "soft" panel using fabric store materials such as cotton reels and trimmings.

Each individual number contains two materials but, if you are making up a larger composite panel like this one, you must also give careful consideration to the positioning of each element so that the whole piece balances. Some of the materials were clearly more suitable for particular numbers: for instance, the "8" with its coils and the "4" with its straight lines. These formed fixed points in the panel around which the other materials could be arranged. The bottle caps and broken ceramic panels were added because a wide range of colors were available from which an appropriate selection could be made that would balance the whole.

An MDF panel was painted in different colors for each section and the elements were laid out loose on paper before being transferred individually and fixed in position. (See the "Found Objects Panel" on pages 62–3, and page 114 for full instructions.) This was done because a large area of adhesive was going to be visible between the pieces and it was difficult to think of a color that would be sympathetic to all the different materials used. The solution was to use a transparent silicone through which the painted backgrounds would show. Silicone was also a practical choice of adhesive as it is very flexible and would stand up to the extreme changes in temperature experienced inside a conservatory.

0 This section is made of colored marbles set into clear marbles. The shapes are identical and the reflectivity very similar so the number is only distinguished by the flashes of colored glass. The similarity of the two materials makes a subtle effect.

1 The number is formed from bright pink buttons set against vivid green tap washers; the background is dark buttons laid in rows. There is variety in the size and color of the buttons and the contrast between dark and bright is strong enough to mark out the "1". There is a dynamic contrast between the vertical pink row and the horizontal dark rows.

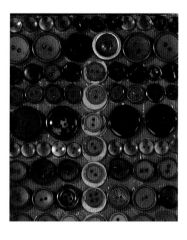

2 Fragments of broken mirror are surrounded by pieces of shattered safety glass. The mirror was chosen to match the thickness of the glass and, while both materials have a depth to them, the silvered backing of the mirror shines out in contrast to the translucence of the glass.

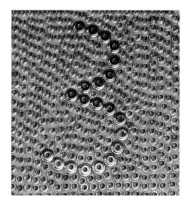

3 The "3" is made of silvered washers set against a sea of tiny brass eyelets. The two materials share a metallic reflectivity although they are different in both size and color. The eyelets were a particularly successful find as they are sold in large quantities and have a very pleasing degree of variation in color.

4 The background is made up of copper clips that are used to fix copper water pipes to a wall. The number is formed with plastic electrical connector strip. Both materials stand out a similar distance from the board and the little metal screws inside the connectors provide a metallic twinkle that relates to the glossy copper hoops.

5 This panel is made of glazed ceramic pieces with the number picked out in a darker tone. These particular tiles are no longer manufactured and we were given them by someone clearing out their garage. Although they would be hard to track down they are the sort of treasure that is often carefully preserved in a biscuit tin or jam jar. Irregular broken fragments of bathroom tiles could be used to create a similar effect.

6 Bottle caps make excellent mosaic materials as they are available in such a wide variety of colors and designs but all in the same size and thickness. If you are not a big drinker you can always ask your local bar to set some caps aside for you. Small holes in the design can be filled with half caps that can be cut with ordinary scissors then straightened up with pliers. (Use an old pair of scissors as cutting will blunt them.)

7 Both background and number are made of broken ceramic tiles, with the brighter fragments used to form the "7". The tiles are glazed terracotta and the rich burnt orange sides are glimpsed in the joints.

8 Brilliant green plastic rope has been used for both figure and background. When rope comes off a coil it is difficult to straighten out so the "8" was the perfect figure to make out of this natural spiral. The background rope came in a hank and consequently had straight sections that could be cut into strips.

9 The figure is made of circular ceramic tiles and the background of a variety of yellow buttons. Because the background is so mottled the figure is clearer for being formed out of a different material. However, the visual difference of having no holes is very subtle and the identical circular shape creates a strong relationship between the two materials.

10 As with "0" this panel is made of marbles, but here the figure is picked out in opaque clay marbles. Some of these have a reflective metallic finish that relates to the reflective surface of the glass marbles and they are of identical size and shape. The variety of different marbles in the figures is a product of necessity as there were not enough of any single type. This kind of difficulty can always be turned to advantage by creating combinations that produce more variety and interest.

ENTRANCE PORCH

This design was made for the front porch of a house in a leafy suburb. The front garden is lushly planted and beautifully tended and the street is lined with a variety of ornamental trees. This environment of nature under beneficent and humane control is reflected in the design of the mosaic. The lively animals and fish are shown against a formal background of stylized land and water. The "land" is laid in a fan pattern and is a reference to more traditional entrance floors. Equally the water is laid in a very simplified and stylized wave pattern (see "Water" on page 49). The overall effect is to make the viewer uncertain whether they are looking at a decorative pattern or a naturalistic scene, and this ambiguity makes the piece more interesting than it might be if it was straightforwardly either abstract or pictorial.

Unglazed ceramic was chosen for the floor because of its hard-wearing properties. The muted colors are also sympathetic to the subtle greens in the front garden. The mounds or fans have touches of the green glass that is the reverse side of gold tiles and the waves are enlivened with flashes of mirror. The background is made up of quarter-cut tiles

while the creatures are made of larger pieces, which helps to bring them forward and separate them from the patterns behind. The treatment of the animals and fish is quite simplified, concentrating on their overall shape and markings, rather than engaging in shading and three-dimensional modelling. Nonetheless their brighter colors stand out strongly against the more muted background and their attitudes, particularly those of the fish and reptiles, give a suggestion of movement and liveliness.

The decorative panel is surrounded by an area of plain green mosaic. It is a good idea to give a design a plain frame if you are abutting existing walls as they will almost always be slightly out of square. This will be less noticeable in a plain area than it would be if you had to cut into the decorative area. Framing is also a useful strategy if the walls are interrupted with columns or recesses because it will enable you to make an elegant rectangular panel without drawing

attention to the irregular perimeter. One important consideration when designing a porch floor is the orientation of the piece. At front doors it is the convention that any decoration or lettering is orientated outward for the benefit of the visitor. There may be circumstances, however, when it would be better to orientate inward, for instance when the floor is overlooked from a favorite spot within the house.

Whatever you are making in mosaic the lines of laying are a very important consideration, both in terms of the ease of execution and the finished appearance. Where you are covering a considerable area in a single color the laying technique assumes an even greater importance as the pattern of grout lines will be very dominating and should be carefully selected to create an effect that enhances the mosaic.

LAYING

DIRECTIONAL

In illustrations 1, 2 and 3, the pieces are laid along lines. These continuous grout joints will read more strongly than the intermediate joints and will therefore emphasize the lines of laying.

1 The white is laid in straight horizontal lines, which make the egg look very flat. It would not be practical to lay this shape in vertical lines as the edge rows would have to be made of very small pieces which would be difficult to achieve. In contrast, the background is laid to the curve of the egg's outline to create a lively effect and emphasize the white shape.

2 A slightly curved line has been chosen for the white area, which gives the shape an almost three-dimensional quality. This effect is heightened by being set against a background that is laid in straight horizontal lines that create a much flatter appearance. Laying in parallel lines gives a calm and orderly effect and is usually the least obtrusive technique to use. It can also help in emphasising lines of movement, for instance of water in the backgrounds of marine scenes.

3 Further emphasis can be added by using rectangular rather than square pieces. The long thin shapes laid across the egg create a strong horizontal effect in contrast to the vertical laying of the background.

NON-DIRECTIONAL

It is difficult to choose an appropriate line of laying for some projects. You may not wish to emphasize one particular direction; it may be that lines in all directions would be interrupted, resulting in a lot of awkward cutting. Illustrations 4, 5 and 6 demonstrate techniques that create an overall effect of a uniform pattern of grout lines across the surface.

4 The tiles are laid to a grid of lines running in both directions, which is occasionally interrupted by half and quarter tiles laid within the structure of the main grid. These help to make the small cut pieces at the edge of the white shape less obvious but nonetheless the cutting around the outline is very fiddly and the result a much less elegant curve than in the other examples. It is a very unforgiving technique and works best with straight lines.

5 This piece demonstrates a method of laying using random sized pieces which is much more flexible and can be applied to the most awkward of shapes. Within the egg there are some angled cuts that set the tiles off in different directions, while in the background all the pieces are roughly square or rectangular and laid parallel to the edges of the piece. The pattern of grout lines is thus quite busy and unpredictable and provides a way of making the surface interesting while maintaining a very flat overall effect.

6 This example demonstrates the use of more orderly patterns, which can be introduced to give large single colored areas interest in a more structured and therefore calmer way.

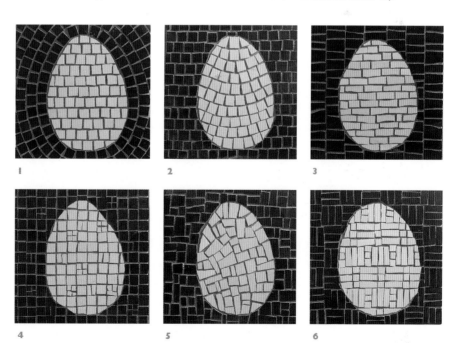

1 2 3

4 5 6

ECHO AND NARCISSUS

This framed panel illustrates the Greek story of Echo and Narcissus. Echo was punished by the gods for her continual chattering by having her powers of speech reduced to the repetition of the last word uttered in her presence. Unable to declare her love for Narcissus, Echo fled to the mountains to live in the caves that she inhabits to this day, condemned to repeat words back to her visitors forever. In the mosaic, Echo is seen running along a path through an imaginary landscape that leads to the hills. Narcissus was himself punished by falling in love with his own reflection and, unable to drag himself away from his mesmerising image, he died of starvation. Here he is shown gazing into the fountain in the center of a walled garden where he will eventually perish and be transformed into the flower that bears his name and which flourishes beside springs and pools.

This mosaic panel is inspired by classical, Byzantine and medieval sources that have influenced the approach to composition, narrative content and decorative treatment. The composition is essentially flat with both buildings and the ground behind them expressed without perspective or foreshortening. In this way the horizontal surface of the garden occupies the same plane as the vertical walls of the buildings and as the distant hills. This unifies the different elements of the design and allows them all to be treated as patterned surfaces. However, they are also separated by a dark background that allows each "patch" to work as an individual composition.

Across the whole picture the components are carefully balanced with bright and dark areas represented either side of the central garden panel, and the pale gray of the hills at the top repeated in the path at the bottom. The garden itself is slightly off center, which helps draw the eye to the figure of Echo who is positioned directly across from Narcissus to indicate the narrative connection between them. In this piece the story is not told in the bold style of the medieval mosaicists as it is not intended as a didactic polemic against the vices of vanity or too much chattering. Instead the actions of the figures are secondary to the overall composition and have to be sought out like clues in a puzzle. It is a technique famously used by Brueghel in his picture of Icarus falling to earth where the foreground is taken up with a scene of peasants and oxen, oblivious of the tiny figure plunging into the sea behind them. Stories of human vanity and frailty are perhaps given an added poignancy when set in the larger context of the ordinariness of everyday life. The figures and animals are very simply rendered as the scale of the piece cannot allow great detail. They are

animated by the use of dark and light tiles to indicate some shading and are shown as if arrested in motion rather than standing stiffly against their more static backgrounds.

The garden and the fields are laid to precise repeating patterns to convey the carefully tended land. This is in contrast to the dark background and the sky which are laid in a more random way that avoids setting up any dominant lines of direction. This is important because it helps to create an even surface that reinforces the overall flatness of the piece. Because the composition is quite busy the palette used is relatively limited, but interesting effects are created by using the same colors in different combinations. For example, the two top fields both contain the same purple but used with green in one and brown in the other and because the colors are close in tone they merge together and create two distinct effects. It is a way of creating new colors that are not available as individual tiles, rather as the impressionists created colors with strokes of different colors rather than mixing them together. The effect is one of great vibrancy.

Because of the complexity of this piece it was made using the indirect method. This allowed revisions to be made to insure that the finished piece balanced and the figures and animals were not completely invisible. It was fixed with a cement-based adhesive onto an MDF board because it is designed to be hung indoors. It has been grouted in two colors because of the extreme contrast between the garden and buildings and the dark background. The whole piece was pregrouted in gray and the garden and buildings then regrouted and the piece sponged clean. Using rubber gloves, dark gray grout was then applied to the background and to the dark fields and this was then carefully sponged off to avoid smearing the gray areas. This is easier with a small piece of sponge, but excess grout in the wrong place can be washed off without difficulty while it is still wet. A little bit of dark grout has also been added to the figures to help give them definition against their pale backgrounds, and similarly the gray/brown animals have been left gray grouted against their dark fields.

Many of the points raised here are covered elsewhere in the book, but this is a summary of the problems and virtues of using color in a garden. The examples given here illustrate the principle that color is not a single unchanging entity.

Its appearance depends partly on surface – whether or not a material is reflective or matte, textured or smooth – but also on a relationship with the colors around it. Do not underestimate the determining influence grout can have on the appearance of color. As a general rule, match the grout color to the principal tone of the mosaic.

When plants die back and there are no intensely colored flowers to counterbalance a bright design, a vibrantly colored mosaic may become isolated and seem less successful in its surroundings. To avoid this problem select a palette that relates to the brick, stone or building materials of your house, walls or paths. You are less likely to tire of a mosaic like Icarus (below) that has a harmonious relationship with its surroundings, and a limited palette doesn't have to be boring, as you can see.

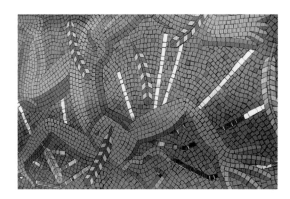

The theme of the mosaic below unites the natural world and the kitchen. It depicts the smallest of culinary ingredients – a peppercorn, a grain of rice, a chilli pepper and so on. The scale is humorous and the tiles help to bring color to an otherwise featureless wall. Note how tonal color is used in a stylized way to suggest shadows.

Color can be used to make something lively of a dark or dreary spot, but it can also be used in among vegetation. The palette for the Bridge (left) was selected with the blues and greens of its surroundings in mind.

MOSAIC MATERIALS

Marble A polished marble tile has three faces: the polished, glassy face; the rough sawn face, and the riven (or broken) internal face. The internal color of a marble is difficult to determine by looking at the sawn face as saw marks leave the cubes with a whitish finish. The riven face exposes the natural color of the marble and has a textured finish. Each of these finishes has its uses: polished or sawn face material is best for paving, riven marble more suitable for walls. The differences between them are marked when the material is dry. Wetting them makes them all look similar by heightening the intensity of color.

Unglazed ceramic This is one of the cheapest and most durable of mosaic materials and is produced in earthy, neutral tones. Ceramic tiles are the same on both sides, so if you make an inaccurate cut, you can often turn the tile over and start again. Ceramic focuses attention on the way the material is laid, which can be a disadvantage if your cutting is not a hundred per cent accurate.

Vitreous glass These factory made tiles in glass paste are probably the most popular form of mosaic and offer the widest range of colors. "Gemme" are glass tiles striated with metallic ore. They have a coppery or gold streaked appearance. Glass can be very effective used with ceramic.

Stained glass Opaque stained glass can be cut with a score-and-snap glass cutter and made into glass tesserae. It should not be used underfoot.

Smalti Smalti, the high-fired enamelled glass made in and around Venice, is one of the oldest of mosaic materials. It is intensely colored, which can make it difficult to use subtly. However, if you need a material capable of standing up to the muting effects of distance, smalti is ideal. Closer to, it can be effective used in combination with marble.

Gold, silver and metallic mosaic The the metal is sandwiched between two layers of glass. The finest metal-faced mosaic is probably Italian. For wall-quality gold, silver and a range of other metals, the material is often backed with colored glass. Floor-quality material (pavimento gold or silver) is fixed on clear glass so you can look through to the metal finish below. The reflective qualities can make these tiles difficult to use effectively on a small scale. Used generously, they can look opulent and fabulous, but at a fabulous price.

THE MARBLE WORKSHOP

Marble has been used in mosaic-making for centuries. Recently there has been a resurgence of interest in its natural properties, but it is not easy to learn how to use it. Firstly, if a supplier stocks marble mosaic at all it is generally in ready-to-lay designs, sheeted up on paper or laid on mesh. Secondly, there is a degree of protectionism among mosaicists who are keen to discourage amateurs from learning the secrets of their trade. If you wish to use it for yourself though, this section aims to help.

Unless you can afford to lay out a considerable sum, learn how to scavenge. Masons' yards and tile shops normally have scrap bins and – the best source of all – marble suppliers often have plenty of discarded material. Broken tiles, small scraps and off-cuts are an invaluable resource. The basic marble-cutting tools (tile nippers, a mosaic hammer and a hardy) are fairly pricey, so it will help to economize on materials. In addition to the basics tools, you will need a mask and protective eyewear.

Apart from tools and materials, the essentials in a marble workshop are good light and ventilation. It is as important to see the color of the tiles as it is to use the space tidily and rationally. We store marble cubes in plastic pots and marble rods in the polystyrene boxes that they come in from the supplier. We generally sort material by color and cube size. It is useful to have scrap bins for off-cuts, as almost no piece of marble is too small to be useable. Buy a couple of large plastic stackable bins and push them under a work-bench when not in use.

There is a big difference between using ready formed marble cubes and producing your own. Whatever tools you use, the aim should be

to make tesserae of a similar size. It is possible to use tiles of varying sizes, but this limits the ways of laying the material. Different sizes require careful sorting, or have to be laid in a random way.

Some kinds of marble are suitable for exterior use, others are not. Ask your mason or supplier for advice about the materials he is prepared to let you have. It is frustrating to put an enormous amount of effort into making a mosaic only to have it change color or fail.

CHAPTER 7
TECHNICAL INFORMATION

Although external mosaics are common in southern Europe they are found less frequently further north where they are generally limited to front steps and shop entrances, often sheltered by a porch or canopy. You will also find wall mosaics in lunettes above the west doors of churches, again often protected by an overhang. The reason for this relative scarcity is that, as with all building techniques, the northern climate presents far greater technical challenges. It is always a surprise for northeners to see so many half-finished buildings in the Mediterranean, left open to the elements from season to season as the owners await the right moment to continue, without any sense of urgency or fear of continued deterioration. While this is partly a matter of temperament it is also a reflection of a kinder climate.

In the north, the climate is wet and there is a far greater variation in temperature, both between night and day and between seasons. Worst of all are the low winter temperatures and the perils of frost and ice. The mosaic fixers of Italian origin like to maintain that external mosaics north of the Alps are completely impractical, but this may be because they also have to suffer the discomforts of working outdoors in less than idyllic conditions. In fact it is possible to fix durable mosaics outside so long as appropriate materials and techniques are used. Listed below are some potential pitfalls and suggested ways of avoiding them.

COMMON PROBLEMS

Rot

This problem will not affect mosaic materials themselves but can damage timber backings and frames. Most grout is slightly porous and even completely waterproof epoxy grouts may develop small holes or cracks allowing ingress of water to the backing material. This is a particular problem with horizontal surfaces such as table bases where the water will not drain away. Even on vertical panels it may collect in pockets or be held in by the frame. Untreated timber will rot quite quickly if it is permanently wet or damp, so it is essential when using timber backings outdoors to specify an exterior grade timber, plywood or MDF.

Frost

The problems of water penetration described above are exacerbated by cold temperatures. Trapped water can freeze and the resulting expansion will push a mosaic away from its backing. This can happen regardless of the type of backing material used and it is therefore advisable to eliminate cavities behind the mosaic in exterior work. When fixing with thin-bed adhesive this is done by "solid-bedding", which can be achieved either by pressing down very hard on the adhesive and squeezing out the trowel notches or by buttering the back of the mosaic with a thin layer of adhesive that will bond with the trowelled layer to form a slightly thicker bed. When fixing into a sand/cement bed the problem does not arise as the mosaic is beaten into the bed.

Slime

This is a problem that can affect underwater mosaics and mosaics that are wet for long periods. The algae that flourish in water, when accompanied by sunlight, come in various forms: some are obviously plant-like, others appear as a uniform green film. One of our clients was adamant that the glass mosaics themselves were losing their color, gradually dissolving into the water, but it transpired that all the color changes were due to a thin coat of green slime. Algae can be effectively scrubbed off with a scouring pad and some elbow grease and there are proprietary products that can be added to the water to inhibit growth. These are designed for use in fish tanks and are therefore not threatening to wildlife, but if your fountain or pond is uninhabited the stronger chemicals used in swimming pools would be more effective.

Salts

These are a crusty white powdery residue, not unlike table salt, that can form on the surface of many externally used materials, such as brickwork and mosaic. The effect is caused as water rises through the backing material and evaporates on contact with the air, leaving a deposit of impurities crystallized on the surface.

(The same effect can be observed when wet shoes are left to dry out. The characteristic white "tide-mark" is particularly marked in snowy weather when there is salt on the roads.) The problem can be avoided by insuring that the backing wall or surface is properly dry before fixing. Render and concrete must be left approximately one week for every 1 inch of thickness. Surfaces that are permanently damp, such as retaining walls or slabs laid over water-logged ground, are not suitable for decoration with mosaic.

Thermal movement

All materials expand as they get hotter and contract as they get colder. In an outdoor environment rapid temperature changes occur between full sun and shadow and there are slower but more extreme variations between day and night temperatures and winter and summer conditions. Problems can arise when the mosaic covering moves at a different rate from the material behind. This is particularly severe if the backing is metal as its high co-efficient of expansion means that it moves a lot and can cause the adhesive to shear and the mosaic to crack. It can also be a serious problem with glass, which is so brittle that it can fracture under quite small stresses. To avoid this it is necessary to use a very flexible adhesive that can absorb the different rates of movement without losing grip on either surface. Silicone is suitably flexible for use on glass and there are proprietary products such as Bal-Flex that are cement based with latex additives for use on metal.

With all mosaic and backing materials it is important to leave sufficient space between the pieces to allow expansion and contraction to take place; because mosaic pieces are so small and the joints so many, this need be only a fraction. Over a certain distance, generally 10 to 13 feet, movement accumulates and it is necessary to introduce special straight joints that run through both the mosaic and the backing and that can be filled with a waterproof and flexible silicone or mastic. These movement joints must also be made where there are junctions in the backing material, for instance between timber boards or between boards and brickwork.

Structural movement

If the backing material is not rigid, movement will occur due to vibration and knocking and this may cause the adhesive to fail. With timber backings such as plywood, large thin sheets will not only have a tendency to bend when moved but also to warp when exposed to damp conditions. Backs of boards should always be sealed or made as weatherproof as possible so that there are no extreme differences of water absorption between back and front faces which will cause warping (the ideal solution for large panels is to fix plain mosaic to the back so that the faces are perfectly balanced). Bracing timbers can also be screwed to the back diagonally and to the edge to stiffen the panel. Metal panels can be strengthened in a similar way using metal angle struts.

Sand and cement backings, whether walls or floors, will only be as stable as their sub-base: crumbling brickwork and subsiding or shrinking ground will cause the covering to crack. It is always a good idea to reinforce sand and cement, using stainless steel expanded metal lathing in wall render and galvanized metal mesh in floor slabs, to give the covering some independent tensile strength.

The central lesson to be learned from these various problems is that weather is the enemy! If you make relatively small pieces and live in an exposed area it may be worth bringing the mosaics in over the winter. If you are making a permanent piece on a wall or floor you may be able to select a sheltered spot, for instance close to the house where temperatures will remain a little higher, or on a north-facing wall where direct sunlight will not be a problem. Wherever you choose you should always assume that some movement may occur and lay the mosaic with adequate joints and use an adhesive that allows for some flexibility. So long as all your mosaic, backing and fixing materials are water- and frost-proof, your mosaic should survive the elements without difficulty. After all, mosaics have survived from the Roman era, fixed into the highly flexible medium of lime mortar, and they have moved and settled without fragmenting. It is worth remembering that the cracking and crumbling at the edges found in ancient mosaics by no means spoils the overall effect and that if a few minor defects appear over a period of time they will simply add to the character of your mosaic.

MATERIALS

Backings

Boards: suitable for wall panels and tabletops The options are: marine ply (high specification to withstand salt water); exterior-grade ply; exterior MDF, which is more stable than ply; mineral boards such as "Master board" or "Pyroc" are heavy but very stable and durable. Note that mineral board is difficult to cut, often blunting saw blades.

Large panels need thick boards to prevent flexing. Thinner boards can be braced with treated softwood battens. Edges may be vulnerable but hardwood beading can be glued and pinned to the edge of ply and MDF boards, and aluminium angle can be used with boards of all materials. Remember that all fixings must be rust-proof (brass, stainless steel or galvanized).

Sand and cement: suitable for walls (render) and floors (screeds) New sand and cement backings should be reinforced with stainless steel or galvanized mesh and allowed to dry out completely before fixing. Existing surfaces should be sound, dry and clean. Cement-based adhesives will stick to painted surfaces, but the bond between the render and the paint must be sound and all flaking areas removed. If a thin-bed adhesive is being used, the surface must be flat as bumps and hollows will be seen in the finished mosaic. Lumps can be rubbed off with a grinding stone and hollows filled with cement-based adhesive.

The edges of the mosaic may be vulnerable and can be protected in various ways: proprietary tile trims can be bedded into the adhesive giving a neat metal up stand. Bricks and pavers should be laid flush to the surface of a floor mosaic with a grout joint between.

Placing marble nosings (strips of marble at least 4 inches wide) at the leading edge of stair treads is the best way to protect mosaic steps.

Mesh: suitable for walls and floors Plastic tile-backing mesh can be used for both wall and floor mosaics as an intermediate layer between the mosaic and the backing, although this is never as reliable a method as either direct or indirect fixing. Organic meshes such as hessian are unsuitable for outdoor use as they will rot. The tiles can be glued to the mesh with an aliphatic wood glue, such as Titebond. A plastic sheet should be placed under the mesh to prevent the mosaic sticking to the table below. When the glue is dry the completed sections can be fixed with a cement-based adhesive. Where the mosaic is complicated and made up of small pieces the indirect method is best.

Metal: suitable for tabletops Steel can be galvanized or powder-coated to protect it and some metals, such as aluminium and stainless steel, will not deteriorate outside. During fabrication of steel table bases, spot-welding can distort the base plate so care must be taken to achieve a level surface. Because metal expands and contracts, a flexible adhesive must be used.

Terracotta and concrete: suitable for pots and paving slabs Planters and slabs can be used as mosaic backings. Porous surfaces should be primed with dilute PVA before fixing with cement-based adhesive.

Plastic Plastic objects are not generally rigid enough to be covered in mosaic. Some shapes such as spheres or pipes help to increase stiffness, but a highly flexible adhesive should be used to accommodate thermal movement.

TECHNICAL INFORMATION

Adhesives and grouts

Sand and cement These are the traditional materials for all mosaic fixing on both walls and floors. A mix of 3:1 or 4:1 is laid in a thin bed of ½ to 1 inch), depending on the thicknesses of the materials used, and the mosaic is beaten into the screed to form a flat surface. For large areas this is a very skilled job as each section has to level through with the adjoining pieces and it is generally best left to professional fixers. For smaller pieces that can be fixed in two or three sections it is quite manageable and provides a useful method where materials of different thicknesses have been used and a flat surface is required. White or gray Portland cement should be used and sharp washed sand.

Cement-based adhesive These are proprietary tiling adhesives based on the traditional mixture of sand and cement but enhanced with modern chemical additives. Some are designed specifically for exterior work and can be used for both the direct and indirect or reverse methods. Different manufacturers' products will have different properties so it is important to study the instructions carefully and consult companies' technical departments with specific enquiries. Adhesives with different setting speeds are available, as are two-part adhesives with highly flexible characteristics such as Bal-Flex.

Polyvinyl acetate (PVA) PVA is a white liquid glue that comes in various degrees of permanence. For sticking mosaic materials to paper in the indirect method, you will need washable or water-soluble PVA that dissolves when wet. To check what kind of PVA you have, stick down one or two tiles on paper, leave them to dry then try to soak them off.

Irreversible PVAs, such as Unibond, can be used in the direct method to stick mosaic materials to boards so long as these are kept indoors.

Aliphatic wood glues These are liquid yellow glues, such as Titebond, that are easy to work with and waterproof. They can be used to stick mosaic materials to both mesh and timber.

Silicone This is a thick jelly-like glue that comes in various colors, including translucent, and is available from most hardware stores. It is generally sold in cartridges for mastic guns or in small tubes. Absolutely clear silicone is also available from specialist glaziers. Its translucence and flexibility make it suitable for sticking glass to glass, but it can be used for sticking most impervious surfaces where serious thermal or structural movement is expected. It can be quite messy to use but any excess can be washed off with a scourer and some water before it dries. It is very difficult to remove afterwards. The glue is water-resistant so the materials to be bonded must be dry.

Epoxy These are two-part resin-based adhesives and grouts. Some manufacturers make them as separate products while some are combined. As with silicone, these materials are quite tricky to use as they can only be cleaned with a scouring pad and clean water before they set and so fixing must be carried out in small areas at a time. The advantages of epoxy are that it is as flexible and strong as an adhesive and as waterproof as a grout.

Cement-based grout Grout is a weak mix of sand and cement (i.e. mostly sand) used to fill the joints between tiles to allow movement without cracking. It is available in a range of colors and can also be tinted with proprietary colorizers. Depending on the size of the aggregate or sand particles used, grouts are classified as suitable for narrow and wide joints. In practice you may find that although the coarser grouts do not fill the joints flush with the surface they are considerably easier to clean off. If you are left with a residue of grout on the surface of the mosaic, clean it off with a dilute acid sold in builders' merchants as mortar cleaner.

Sealants

Stone sealant This is recommended to reduce staining of natural stone and marble mosaic. It is particularly useful for tables, which may be subjected to red wine, oil and coffee spillages that can penetrate untreated marble.

Grout sealant This is recommended for table tops where a cement-based grout has been used. With most materials, the sealant can be applied over the whole surface, left for a few moments to sink into the joints, then washed off. However, some very porous materials may be affected by sealants, so test a small area first.

Silicone sealant Silicone can be used to fill joints that will be subjected to a lot of movement. It is advisable to mask the surfaces on both sides with masking tape before applying silicone, and smoothing it down with a finger.

TOOLS

Tile nippers

Nippers can be used to cut and shape small pieces of all mosaic materials. To cut brittle materials, such as glass and ceramic, the nippers should be placed on the edge of the tile and not all the way across, to avoid shattering. Nippers are now available with two circular blades (made by Leponit) for use with vitreous glass and smalti. They give a very accurate cut.

Tile cutter

This tool is useful for scoring and snapping larger tiles into small pieces or strips that can be shaped by the nippers. For larger and thicker tiles, stronger cutters are available where the scoring wheel and snapper are mounted on a long arm to give greater leverage.

Hammer and hardy

These are the traditional mosaic-cutting tools, probably used in Roman times. Today the hammers have tungsten tips and are brought down on the material as it rests on the hardy, which is an upturned chisel embedded in a tree-trunk or concrete base. This creates a distinctive hand-cut fracture and is the easiest way of cutting some hard natural stones. Today their use is more nostalgic than practical.

Glass cutter

The sharp wheels of a glass cutter scores lines into stained and mirrored glass. The glass can then be snapped by the snapper on a tile cutter or by hand by holding it close to the score line with pliers and snapping it with finger and thumb on the other side of the line. Glass cutters can also be used to score gold and silver tiles to give more accurate cuts.

Grouting squeegees

Various tools are available for grouting. A small plastic comb and blade is suitable for small jobs; use a rubber blade squeegee for intermediate jobs, such as tabletops. Flat-bed squeegees are essential for large jobs, such as pavements and murals.

Trowels

Choose a trowel to fit the job:

3mm notched trowel This is the standard ¼ inch mosaicist's trowel for the application of thin-bed cement-based adhesive to all types of backings. Remember that for external work it is important that the ridges should be completely flattened by pushing the mosaic down into the adhesive and eliminating any cavities.

V-notched trowel Designed for linoleum fixing, this configuration is useful for fixing mosaics with very small pieces as there is less adhesive-free surface area.

Solid-bed trowel This is a ⅛ inch trowel with ¼ inch teeth at either end leaving a thicker bed into which the mosaic can be beaten. This is an effective tool for eliminating cavities but it can be difficult to achieve a flat surface.

Small plastic comb This is useful for small jobs where a trowel will not fit.

Plasterer's small tool This small metal modelling tool is invaluable for applying adhesive to both flat and curved surfaces when using the direct method.

DIRECT ONTO A FLAT SURFACE

Materials

Brown paper

Charcoal pencil

Tracing paper

Pencil

½ inch marine ply

Acrylic paint

Brushes

Silicone

Mastic gun

Grout spreader

1 When working direct onto a flat surface, work out in detail what you intend to do before sticking the pieces down. To do this, make a paper template of the right size, draw on the design then trace it onto tracing paper so that you can transfer it exactly onto the board. You can then try combinations on the paper before making any irrevocable decisions.

2 When using a variety of materials, some may be difficult to cut or look better used whole. This will determine the exact dimensions of the areas covered. Equally, some components may be limited so you will have to lay them out to establish how large an area they will cover. When you have laid out the whole piece, measure the sizes of the panels and adjust the tracing.

3 The outlines of the boxes can be traced onto the board then painted in colors that are sympathetic to the chosen materials. (We used acrylics because they are opaque and available in a wide range of colors.) The numbers were then traced onto the panels. Remember that the glue is transparent so the drawing should be as faint as possible so as not to show through.

4 Carefully transfer the pieces from the paper to the board. Apply a continuous line of silicone backwards and forwards across one colored panel with the mastic gun then spread it across the surface with a grout spreader. (Silicone will stick to any dry, painted surface.) Thin materials such as buttons will need a thinner bed than thicker objects such as marbles or bottle caps. The surface should be as smooth as possible as it may be visible between components. Remember that silicone dries quickly when exposed to the air – within about ten minutes, depending on the air temperature – so do not work on more than one panel at a time.

Other projects

Direct onto a flat surface The Number Panel is intended to hang in a conservatory, but the technique described above can be used equally well with materials suitable for outdoor use. Projects executed in this way are the Found Objects Panel (see page 62) and Charybdis (page 64).

Direct onto a three-dimensional surface Projects executed in this way are the Mosaic Head (page 78) and the Mythical Animal (page 81).

DIRECT ONTO A THREE-DIMENSIONAL SURFACE

Materials

Terracotta planter

Brown paper

Pencil

Scissors

Nippers

Brush

Water-soluble PVA

Palette knife

Exterior cement-based adhesive

Rubber gloves

Grout

Sponge

Lint-free cloth

1 When covering a relatively simple shape that curves in one dimension only, make a paper template first and work out your design on a flat surface. Measure the height of the pot and cut out a long strip of paper of that width. Offer this up to the pot and wrap it around allowing at least ¼ inch overlap to account for the thickness of the mosaic and adhesive bed. Use the edge of the paper to set up a vertical line down the side of the pot.

2 Lay out the tiles on the paper pattern, working out sequences of colors and interlocking patterns. You can also adjust the spacings to avoid a row of ugly cuts either at the bottom or where the pattern meets up at the back.

If the object to which you are fixing the tiles is porous, such as terracotta, it is a good idea to seal it to prevent the cement-based adhesive drying out too quickly. This can be done by painting on a 50:50 solution of PVA and water and leaving it to dry.

3 To stick the tiles to the surface, use an exterior cement-based adhesive mixed to a stiff paste and applied with a small tool or palette knife. This mix will have enough "initial grab" to hold the pieces in place on a vertical surface or even upside down on more complicated shapes. After 15 minutes or so the adhesive will begin to skin over so it is important to apply only a small patch at a time. Try to avoid turning the object as you will easily knock off tiles that have just been stuck down. Either place the piece on top of a high stool or table and move around it yourself, or place it on a board that can be turned (revolving cheese boards are particularly useful!).

4 When all the tiles are stuck on and the adhesive is completely dry, the piece can be grouted. For three-dimensional objects this is best done using a hand protected by a rubber glove. Excess grout should be sponged off with the clean face of a sponge wiped diagonally across the line of the joints. A final polish can be given with a lint free cloth when the piece is dry.

INDIRECT OR REVERSE METHOD

Materials

Charcoal pencil

Marker pen

Brown paper

EVA

Bal-Flex or cement-based adhesive

Nippers

Water-soluble PVA

Brush

Squeegee

Rubber gloves

Sponge

Notched trowel

Hammer and board

Lint free cloth

1 Sketch the design onto the matte side of a sheet of brown paper. Do not use a washable pen, as it may stain the ceramic tiles. Lay the tiles out on the paper. Once you are certain of your choices, start to cut the tiles and stick with water-soluble PVA (mixed with water in a 50:50 ratio). If the paper is bubbling or crinkling, you have either added too much water, or are overloading the glue brush. Put the glue on the paper, not the tile, and only on the area immediately around the tile you are laying. If you are fixing to a board, prime it with EVA and water and leave to dry.

2 When the primer is dry, pre-grout the mosaic by spreading the grout across the back of the tiles with a grouting squeegee. (Use a rubber-gloved hand if the mosaic is fragile or if you have varying thicknesses of tiles.) Push grout into the joints, leaving as little on the back of the tiles as possible. Wet the sponge in a bucket of clean water and squeeze it out until it is as dry as you can make it. Draw the sponge across the mosaic, its side as flat to the surface of the mosaic as possible. When you have done this once, turn the sponge. Repeat, using another side, until the mosaic is clean. You may need to rinse the sponge a couple of times. Never use the same side twice. The mosaic should be entirely clean except for the joints between the tiles.

3 Apply adhesive to the board or substrate with a notched trowel. You can be sure you are applying adhesive properly if a scraping sound can be heard as the trowel is pulled across the board. (If you are fixing to a board outside, you must use Bal-Flex two-part adhesive. Normal exterior cement-based adhesive is suitable for all other cement-based surfaces.)

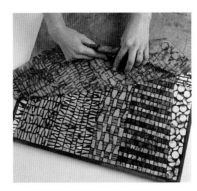

4 Pick up the mosaic and place it into the adhesive tile side down. It is easier to position the mosaic if you pick up diagonally opposed corners. If the fit seems tight, or you have positioned it slightly incorrectly it can be repositioned by beating it into place from the back of the paper. Using a hammer and a small board, tap across the surface, making sure there are no air bubbles. Your aim is to check all the tiles are in direct contact with adhesive. Wet the paper thoroughly with a sponge and do not allow the paper to dry out for at least ten minutes.

5 When the paper has thoroughly absorbed the moisture (it will change color from a light to a dark brown) begin to peel it off. Start by peeling from one corner, in a straight line towards the middle. Flap the paper back down (it will not restick, but if you make a bundle of paper in the middle it has unpredictable consequences on the tiles). Peel in another straight line from the opposite corner. If any tiles come up as you remove the paper simply replace them. This is nothing to worry about and is quite usual, particularly if they are edge tiles. When all the paper has been removed, sponge the surface of the tiles. This is an important task and failure to carry it out has two consequences: the grout may stain the tiles, or it may dry in unsightly patches (like those seen here) on the surface of the tiles.

6 Leave the mosaic to dry and the adhesive to cure before re-grouting. If, as here, the project is small, it is possible to re-grout straight away. Do remember, if you have just peeled off the paper, the mosaic will be extremely fragile. Treat it with care.

7 Sponge off. Remember to turn the sponge and to squeeze as much water out of it as you can. When the mosaic has dried entirely (generally after about 24 hours) buff up the surface with a dry lint free cloth.

Pregrouting

There are two reasons for pre-grouting: the grout acts as a barrier, preventing adhesive squeezing up between the joints and marring the surface appearance of the mosaic. A wet grout is a less effective barrier. Secondly, the grout seems to aid suction so a pregrouted mosaic tends to stay in place better then an ungrouted one. For information on how to make up grout, see step 2 of Casting on page 120.

Other projects

Projects executed with this technique are all the tables in Chapter 1; the Animal Paving Stones (page 27) and the Mosaic Pavement (page 32); the Mosaic Bridge (page 46) and the Fountain (page 52); the Color Wall (page 59) and Icarus (page 66); the Entrance Porch (page 96) and Echo and Narcissus (page 100).

INDIRECT ONTO GLASS

Materials

Brown paper

Nippers

Water-soluble PVA glue

Silicone

Mastic gun

Plastic comb

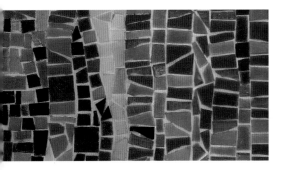

1 When making a translucent panel from vitreous glass it is important to select your colors according to how they look with light shining through them as some colors are completely opaque and others very different in hue. Hold them up to the light to check how translucent they are.

2 In this piece long thin shapes are used made by cutting the tiles into three or even four strips. This made easier by using a special double-wheeled cutting tool made by Leponit that cuts very straight without shattering.

3 Stick the tiles – wrong side facing you – to a square of brown paper cut to the size of the glass. The tiles should be stuck firmly over the whole surface area so that the silicone is contained in the joints and does not spread on to the face. If the piece is insecurely stuck and "crackles" after it has dried, paint another coat of glue onto the face of the paper then turn it over to dry. The glue will penetrate the paper and form a good bond across the full face of the tiles.

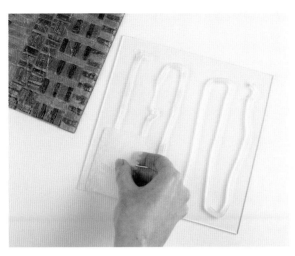

4 When the glass is stuck firmly to the paper, apply a thick bead of silicone across the back of the tiles with a mastic gun. Work it into the joints with a grouting squeegee. Apply silicone in the same way to the sheet of clear glass, spreading it evenly across the surface to form a thin layer of 1/16th inch.

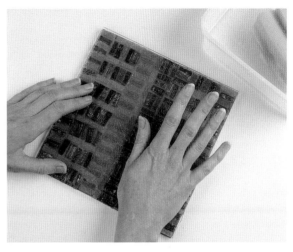

5 The two silicone coated faces should then be immediately pressed together. In a piece of this size it is possible to position the glass sheet on top of the mosaic and apply gentle pressure. You will be able to see through the glass where there is good contact and where air has been trapped and further pressure is required. Don't worry if there are some tiny gaps left as they won't be visible from the other side.

6 Because silicone sticks so well to glass it is difficult to clean off if it gets onto the surface. For this reason it is recommended that you leave the paper on the face until the silicone is completely dry (about four hours). The paper can then be soaked with a wet sponge – it may be necessary to work the water into the paper with the sponge in order to get through any patches of silicone on the paper. When the water-soluble glue has dissolved the paper can be peeled off.

CASTING

Materials

Scissors

Brown paper

Water-soluble PVA glue

Marble cubes (approx. 4 lb cubes at ½ inch thick)

Nippers

Casting frame (or box)

Petroleum jelly

Cloth

2 buckets (one for water, one for sand and cement)

Rubber gloves

Sand

Cement

Sponge

Grout

Expanded metal lath (or galvanized metal mesh)

Wire cutters

Mixing tool (flat ended trowel or wide wallpaper scraper)

Flat bed squeegee or flat bed trowel

Screwdriver

Board to turn over mosaic

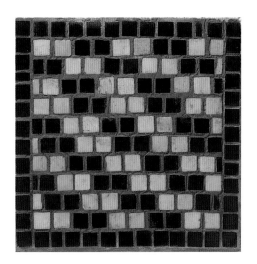

1 Make up the mosaic following step 1 of the indirect method (see page 116). Rub petroleum jelly across the surface of the casting frame, not forgetting edges and corners. This prevents sand and cement sticking to the frame. Place the dry, completed mosaic in the frame.

3 Immerse the sponge in water and squeeze out until it is as dry as possible. Draw the sponge across the surface of the mosaic in one sweep, turn to a different side of the sponge and repeat. When you have used all the sides of the sponge, rinse and repeat until the mosaic is entirely clean.

2 Pre-grout the mosaic with a cement slurry. Place 4 parts sand to 1 part cement in a bucket (a plastic ice-cream container makes a useful measure) and mix thoroughly before adding water (the task is heavier and more laborious once the materials are wet). It is impossible to give precise instructions about how much water to add, as the quantity depends on how wet the sand is. It should not be running with water, or sloppy. The ideal consistency could be described as creamy if it were not so granular. Mix again. Add the same proportions of dry sand and cement if you have over estimated the quantity of water. If this is the first time you have used marble, you may be surprised by how much grout is needed. As a thicker material, marble requires a greater quantity than glass or ceramic.

4 Place a layer of sand and cement on the back of the mosaic. When you are half way up the remaining space lay the metal mesh (which helps to give strength to the sand and cement) and cover with sand and cement until you reach the top of the frame. Push the mixture firmly with a flat bed squeegee (or something similar) making sure all the corners of the frame are filled and the surface is even. Place the frame in a plastic bag for 24 hours. This allows the slab to begin the process of curing and the plastic bag stops it from happening too fast.

5 Unscrew the sides of the casting frame. Timing is crucial here: if you remove the slab from the frame too early, or are not sufficiently careful, you risk cracking it. If, on the other hand, you leave the slab to cure for a long time (a week or so) it can become difficult to remove the paper. This is not generally a problem with glass or ceramic, but can be a problem with marble, particularly unpolished marble, as the surface is absorbent and takes up the glue. We recommend removing the edges of the casting frame, putting a small board on top of the mosaic – now sandwiched between board and casting frame – and turning it over carefully. This allows the paper to be removed while it is still wet: a much easier task now than later. (See next step.)

6 If you are doing this process within 24 hours of having made the slab, the paper may still be wet enough to allow you to peel it off immediately. If it has dried out at all, wet and leave for ten minutes before peeling. Regrout the face of the mosaic, sponge off, and leave for a week in a plastic bag again. The surface can then be buffed up, and the slab laid in the garden.

Working with sand and cement

There are no great secrets to working with sand and cement. A mixture of sand and cement on a wall is called a render; a mixture used on a floor is referred to as a screed. Do not make the mistake of describing this mixture as cement, which is the name for the powder, or concrete, which is a very strong and stable mixture of sand, cement and an aggregate such as pebbles. If you refer to it as "sand and cement", builders will understand you.

The most important thing to know about sand and cement is the proportion of each material to mix. A mix with a greater proportion of cement will be stronger, but more brittle, making the mixture more liable to crack. A greater sand content creates a weaker, and sometimes more flexible mix. This is why fine sand may be included in a cement slurry (the creamy mixture of cement and water often used to grout exterior mosaics). There are pros and cons to both strong and weak mixes: a strong mix of 3 parts sand to 1 part cement may withstand foot traffic or even vehicular traffic, but if subjected to intense pressure it may crack. A pressure crack will run along the weakest point, which may well be the mosaic itself. Although we have had to repair mosaics damaged in this way, there is little one can do to prevent it. Like houses, mosaics are subject to pressure and strains, but like them they can be worth the effort involved in maintaining them.

Sometimes people ask us what mosaic was fixed with in the days before cement. It is a good question. The secret ingredient – used extremely widely before the twentieth century – was lime. A mortar which includes lime is flexible and will move without cracking. Areas of mosaic fixed into a lime-free cement mortar are hard, making repairs difficult. So why do we not use lime now? The answer is that we probably should, but professional fixers are not keen to use it. It can be toxic, it is messy, it takes time to prepare. As mosaicists we are not experienced in using it so we cannot advise you how to do so. Perhaps lime is unpopular because it was associated with an old-fashioned, time-consuming, backward-looking world. If we knew more about it, we might understand its advantages. Let us know if you have personal experience, positive or negative.

MOSAIC INSERTS FIXED INTO SAND AND CEMENT

Materials

Scissors

Brown paper

Water-soluble PVA glue

Nippers

Casting frame (or box)

Petroleum jelly

Baton

Cloth

2 buckets (one for water, one for sand and cement)

Rubber gloves

Sand

Cement

Sponge

Grout

Expanded metal lath (or galvanized metal mesh)

Wire cutters

Mixing tool (flat ended trowel or wide wallpaper scraper)

Flat bed squeegee or flat bed trowel

Hammer

Small board

Screwdriver

Board to turn over mosaic

1 Using the instructions for the Casting (page 120) as a guide, fill the frame half full with the wet mix, lay some galvanized mesh as support for the cast slab, then place more sand and cement on top of it. Lay a well-greased baton into the wet mix, and shake the frame gently to make any water bubbles rise to the surface. Smooth down the surface with a flat trowel then set the slab aside for a couple of days to cure (this process is best done with the slab wrapped up, to slow down the curing process). Remove the baton from the dry slab, as shown here. You might find that some of the sand and cement comes away with it, leaving behind a crumbly edge, so be prepared to undertake repairs. This is tedious, but not difficult to do.

2 Prepare a mosaic strip following step 1 of the indirect method (page 116). With the baton removed, check that the strip fits into the hole. Mix a cement slurry made up of 50:50 cement and fine sand. Fill the hole with the slurry: any excess will squeeze out from the sides.

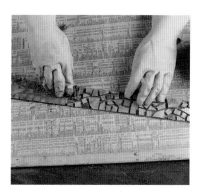

3 The heights of hand-made pavimento gold and silver tiles vary, which makes grouting with a squeegee difficult. Gloved hands are more sensitive, and less likely to inflict damage on the mosaic. Make sure all the joints are filled, and as little remains on the back of the tiles as possible.

4 Although you can pregrout the strip with cement slurry, we preferred the blue-gray color of this grout. Technically both work well, but if you are using grout insure that it is sponged off the back of the tiles, and left only between the joints. (You need not be so meticulous cleaning off a cement slurry, as the fixing bed and the grout are the same.) Wet the sponge, squeeze out until it is as dry as you can make it, and draw it across the tiles in one long sweep. Turn the sponge and repeat the process.

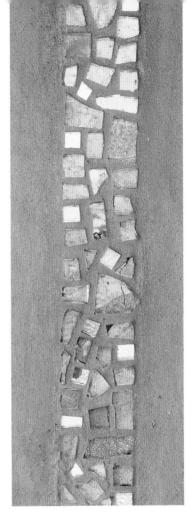

5 Turn over the sponged-off strip and lay it into the slurry-filled groove. Find a light hammer and a small board and work your way down the strip, tapping the mosaic gently. As excess slurry squeezes out from the edges, carefully wipe it away. Repeat this process until the strip is flush with the level of the sand and cement. Wet the paper thoroughly and leave it for ten minutes to absorb the moisture, rewetting if it looks as if it is beginning to dry out.

6 Peel off the paper. If any tiles should come away in the process, simply apply a dab of slurry to the back of them, and tap into position. When all the paper has been removed, carefully sponge the back of the tiles once again, and leave to dry. Twenty-four hours later, regrout and clean off. It your time scale allows, leave the slab in place for another couple of days before removing from the frame and placing into position.

Dealing with large mosaics

Very large mosaics can be fixed in a series of pieces. Turn the mosaic over and scribble across the back. (This can be done before any tiles are stuck in place.) Make a diagram of the back (as this is what you will see as you fix the mosaic) numbering both diagram and brown paper. Draw directional arrows on each section, making sure they point the same way! This will insure an almost identical series of pieces of brown paper are put together correctly.

CONSTRUCTING A THREE-DIMENSIONAL BASE

Materials

Clay

Plaster of Paris

Aluminium mesh

Wire

Wire cutters

Cement-based adhesive

Palette knife

Cut-glass fibers (optional)

1

1 In making a three-dimensional object like the Mosaic Head shown on pages 78–9, creating a suitable sub-base is just as important as the final covering of mosaic. First a plaster mold is made from a clay head, then the plaster cast formed. (The clay head can be used as the base if it is made from an air-drying clay that doesn't crack too much as it hardens. To economise on clay you can make a basic structure or "armature" from bits of wood, metal mesh and newspaper to fill out the general shape.) As you are forming the head try to bear in mind the mosaic covering: simplify the fiddly curves around nostrils and eyes and try to assess the effect of the extra thickness of the mosaic, particularly on the width and length of the nose.

2 The next stage is to mold some wire mesh over the base. Use a fine aluminium mesh and cut two pieces, each large enough to cover half the head. Press one piece onto the front of the head and face, folding it as necessary to follow the contours. You may find that the mesh tears in the hollows of the face, particularly the eye sockets, but you can patch these with small pieces of mesh fixed from the inside with twists of wire. Use the other piece of mesh to mold the back of the head. You can distort the mesh at this stage if you need to – for example, to reduce the width of the nose – and you should complete all necessary patching before re-aligning the two halves and fixing them together with twists of wire. You can also make amendments to the overall shape, for instance changing the hair if you are making a series from a single base and want to introduce elements of variety.

This mesh mold needs to be strong enough to carry the weight of the wet adhesive. Folds in the mesh will help to stiffen it and it is also a good idea to continue the neck down to the base board, adding on the shoulders in separate pieces of mesh, as this allows the load from the head to be carried straight downwards.

2

3 The mesh mold can then be covered in a layer of cement-based adhesive, about ½ inch thick, applied with a plasterer's small tool or a palette knife. This coating will easily cover any unevenness in the mesh and you can do further sculpting during this stage by applying more or less adhesive as required. To insure adhesion to the mesh, work a thin layer into the surface then apply more on top. Cut-glass fibers, available from sculptors' suppliers, can be added to the adhesive to strengthen it. The cement-based adhesive should be frost-proof and when it dries out it will form a rigid shell that is both light and strong. Further layers can be added in places until you are happy with the shape.

Your base is ready to be covered in mosaic. (See pages 78–9.)

Variations and other projects

As with the Mosaic Head, a major part of the Mythical Animal project (see pages 81–3) is the making of the base. The technique is similar but because of the scale of the piece it would not be very practical to make a full-sized clay version. (The finished creature is 5½ feet long and 2½ feet high.)

Instead a clay model was made in order to work out the basic shape. From this, dimensions were taken then scaled up by a factor of five. Another consideration with larger objects is that the mesh alone is not strong enough to carry the weight of the cement and so an internal framework is required. This was made of armature wire which is available from sculptors' suppliers and is both strong and malleable. Taking key dimensions from the model, lengths of wire can be cut and bent to form a skeletal framework with one piece forming the creature's profile and backbone and the others forming ribs at right angles and meeting at a "hoop" around the base. These can all be fixed together at the intersections with galvanized wire.

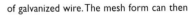

To work out roughly the size and shape of mesh required, clad the model with mesh then flatten it out to position the necessary tucks or "darts" just like a dress-maker's pattern. Key dimensions can then be scaled up and an appropriate shell of mesh formed from four sections: the two sides, the neck and the head. The ears can be made separately. The mesh can be fixed to the framework and to the other sections with twists of galvanized wire. The mesh form can then be covered with a layer of cement-based adhesive ready for the application of mosaic. When you have finished the piece and grouted it you may find that sharp edges are still exposed. Rub these down with fine wet and dry sand paper then sponge off the dusty residue, leaving your creature safe to be stroked and sat on.

SUPPLIERS

Aqua Mix

PO Box 4127
Santa Fe Springs, CA 90670
Phone: 562 946 6877
Website: www,aquamix.com

Supplier of sealants and grouts.

Carter Glass Mosaic Tile

distributed by Hakatai Enterprises, Inc.
695 Mistletoe Rd. Suites C
Ashland, OR 97520
Phone: 888 667 2429
E-mail: hav@hakatai.com
Website: www.hakatai.com

D&L Stained Glass Supply, Inc.

4939 North Broadway
Boulder, CO 80304
Phone: 800 525 0940
Fax: 303 442 3429
Website: www.dlstainedglass.com
E-mail: info@dlstainedglass.com

Delphi Stained Glass

3380 E. Jolly Road
Lansing, MI 48910
Phone: 800 248 2048
Fax: 800 748 0374
Website: www.delphiglass.com
E-mail: sales@delphiglass.com

Mosaic Tile Supply

10427 1/2 Unit A Rush Street
South El Monte, CA 91733
Phone: 626 279 7020
Web site: www.mosaicsupply.com/
E-mail: info@mosaicsupply.com

RL and CO

Phone: 407 739 3399
www.beachglassmosaics.com

Sven Warner-Mountaintop Mosaics

PO Box 653
Elm Street
Castleton, VT 05735
Phone: 800 564 4980
Website: www.mountaintopmosaics.com
E-mail: sven@mountaintopmosaics.com

Wits End Mosaics

Sanford, FL 32771
Phone: 407 323 9122
Fax: 407 322 8552
Website: www.mosaic-witsend.com

PLACES TO VISIT IN THE UNITED STATES AND EUROPE

Exterior mosaics in the USA

NEW YORK

Keep your eyes open as you walk around. New York has spawned a type of mosaic entirely its own. Many shop fronts, sidewalks, entrances and walls are covered with collages of found objects assembled in a lively but formless way. Look at the signs in the subway. These are frequently made in mosaic. New mosaics based on this tradition have recently been commissioned.

Get off the subway at Columbus Circle and walk east. Look up at an apartment building on West 59th Street where there is a series of mosaic murals fairly high up on the building. The composition and subject matter – butterflies, rainbows and factories – have a quirky charm.

Strawberry Fields, Central Park.
A mosaic pavement in memory of John Lennon.

St Mark's Place, East Village.
Ceramic and found object mosaics encrust litter bins and lamp-posts. They were made by the artist Joe Power.

25 Broadway, the Financial District.
These are not exterior mosaics, but interesting nonetheless. The building is based on the Villa Madama in Rome. Now a post office, it used to be the Cunard Booking Office. Mosaics and murals depict sea-scenes, ships, fish, mermaids. It is interesting to see how mosaic is used as part of a decorative scheme.

Facade of William O'Grady High School, Coney Island.
A lively pictorial mural in glass smalti by Ben Shahn.

Irving Trust Company, Wall Street.
The gold and red mosaic in the building's lobby are best seen when the lights are turned on.

Exterior mosaics in the UK

LONDON

The Albert Hall, Kensington Gore.
Nineteenth-century mosaic frieze celebrating the Arts and Sciences.

The Albert Memorial, Hyde Park.
Nineteenth-century series of highly intricate smalti mosaics, some allegorical figures, some patterned.

The Sanderson Hotel, Berners St, W1.
Abstract mosaic panels from the 1960s in the courtyard. See them by visiting the restaurant.

Westminster Cathedral, Victoria.
Nineteenth- and twentieth-century series of smalti mosaics, both inside and outside the building.

The Wharrie Shelter, Haverstock Hill, NW3.
Small glass pavement made for a taxi-rank shelter.

OUTSIDE LONDON

Ashton Memorial, Lancaster, Lancashire.
Pebble mosaic pavement. Designed and made by Maggy Howarth.

Bottle Alley, Hastings, East Sussex.
A series of pre-cast panels of recycled glass in various colours. Post-war. Maker unknown.

Gaze Maze, Riverside walk, Bath, Avon.
1980s marble mosaic depicting scenes from the labyrinth.
Designed by Randoll Coate. Made by Minotaur Designs.

The Little Chapel, St Andrew, Guernsey.
Mosaic made with pebbles and broken crockery. Made by Frere Deodat.

The Shell House, Margate, Kent.
A grotto with a mosaic of shells. Maker unknown.

Summerhouses at West Dean College Gardens, West Dean, Chichester.
Knapped flint and horses' teeth combined in a floor mosaic. Maker unknown.

Tower block fascias, Gosport Seafront.
1950s and 1960s ceramic murals over the sides of two tower blocks. Designed by Kenneth Barden.

Exterior mosaics in Italy

ROME

Pavements at the Foro Italico. A series of black and white marble mosaic pavements show scenes of people at work and at leisure. Some are architectural plans, others are decorative scenes of fish done in a 1930s neoclassical style. The pavements are part of the huge sports complex that Mussolini created when he wanted to host the Olympic Games. Although fascinating, the work is not politically neutral. Artists: Angelo Canevari, Achille Capizzano and Giulio Rosso.

Santa Maria in Trastevere, Trastevere.
Smalti and gold mosaic decorates both the outside and the inside of this interesting church.

Mural on the facade of the Museum of Arts and Crafts, EUR.
A subtly coloured mosaic, combining abstract and representational forms. Artist: Enrico Prampolino.

Ostia Antica
Mosaic pavements are found throughout this Roman archeological site. There are many fabulous black and white mosaics here, including the Baths of Neptune.

TUSCANY

Il Parco dei Tarocchi, Garavicchio.
A sprayed concrete, mirror glass and ceramic piece that is surreal and monumental.

LIGURIA

Promenade, Albisola.
Artists: Mario Rossello, Antonio Siri, Federico Quatrini, Roberto Crippa, Mario Gambetta, Emmanelle Luzzati, Saba Telli, Giuseppe Capogrosso, Wilfredo Lam, Aligi Sassu, Luigi Caldanzano, Mario Porcu, Antonio Franchini, Franco Garalli, Agenore Fabbri, Eliseo Salino, Lucio Fontana, Giambattista de Salvo.
These huge ceramic mosaic pavements were made in the early 1960s.

Mosaics made by Mosaic Workshop

Town Square, Hamilton, Scotland.
A mosaic in opus romano and marble.
Designed by Adrian Wiszniewski.

Mosaic panels for pavements, Seaham, Co. Durham.
Marble mosaic, showing the position of Jupiter and its satellites.
Designed by Susan and Paul Mason.

Marble mosaic roundel, showing the sky above Victoria Park, Hull, Humberside.
Designed by Susan and Paul Mason.

Temple at Goodwood Sculpture Park.
Artist: Allen Jones.
Vitreous glass mosaic figure on top of a temple structure.
Mosaic element made by Mosaic Workshop.

Exterior mosaics by Emma Biggs

A series of mosaic pavements for the Town Square, Wolverton, Bucks.
Designed and made with the children from local schools.

Falkland Gardens, Gosport, Hampshire.
A ceramic mosaic pavement for those lost in the Falklands War and D. Day.

Gosport Esplanade, Hampshire.
Eleven mosaic roundels to commemorate points of local significance.

Timespace Area, Gosport, Hampshire.
A large-scale marble pavement depicting stories of local people and significant events in the history of this naval town. Divided into two sections, past and future.

The Ebbisham Centre, Epsom, Surrey.
Two ceramic mosaic murals based on the Epsom Derby, and the spa history of the town.

Exterior mosaics by Tessa Hunkin

Romford market, Romford, Essex.
Black and white ceramic mosaic depicting local history, buildings and goods sold at the market.

Aerial view mosaic, Shopping Precinct, Horley, Surrey.
A ceramic and glass mosaic pavement showing Horley and surrounding areas, including Gatwick airport.

Mosaic mural for St Marks Hospital, Northwick Park, London.
Vitreous glass abstract background with the lion of St Marks.